Becoming a Mum –
They Didn't Tell Me *That!*

By

Claire D Evans

Published by New Generation Publishing in 2021

Copyright © Claire D Evans 2021

First Edition

The author asserts the moral right under the Copyright, Designs and Patents Act 1988 to be identified as the author of this work.

All Rights reserved. No part of this publication may be reproduced, stored in a retrieval system or transmitted, in any form or by any means without the prior consent of the author, nor be otherwise circulated in any form of binding or cover other than that which it is published and without a similar condition being imposed on the subsequent purchaser.

ISBN
    Paperback   978-1-80031-302-6
    Hardback   978-1-80031-301-9

www.newgeneration-publishing.com

Dedication

For some Mums, having a baby was the hardest thing they've ever done in their lives. For others, it was like 'shelling peas'.

For other Mums, it was the 'getting pregnant' that was the hardest most stressful part. For some, being able to carry the baby full term was the most difficult.

And for a few people I know, trying to get pregnant is the most heart-breaking of all, a constant yearning for children that consumes their lives.

This book is dedicated to all the above.

Acknowledgements

To Garry, Jack and Keira. Without you there would be no book;

To Grandparents Joan, Martin and Sue without whom we would've been well and truly stuck;

To the Aunts and Uncles – and 'adopted' ones too, for taking the kids for us when we needed a break;

To my numerous Mum friends in various circles who helped me remain sane, and for reminding me what friends are for;

And finally, to all the medical professionals in the NHS who helped me in times of need and generally took care of me. You are amazing.

Contents

Chapter 1 - Introduction 1
Chapter 2 – The Freedom 3
Chapter 3 – Married? Kids Yet? 9
Chapter 4 – Success! 16
Chapter 5 – A Breeze! 20
Chapter 6 – A Well Needed Holiday 22
Chapter 7 – Ballooning Nicely 32
Chapter 8 - Worth a Try… 38
Chapter 9 – The Final Stretch 42
Chapter 10 – Ok We're Ready... We Think 49
Chapter 11 – Let's Do It Again! 56
Chapter 12 – A Well *Deserved* Break 66
Chapter 13 – Been There Done That… 72
Chapter 14 – Other Little Pregnancy Gems 78
Chapter 15 – Do This, Do That! 89
Chapter 16 – It's a Hospital, Not a Hotel! 91
Chapter 17 – Sshh –C-Section Secrets 104
Chapter 18 – Reality Hits Home 111
Chapter 19 – Getting the Backside in Gear 115
Chapter 20 – Second Time Differences 123
Chapter 21 – Something's Weighing Heavily 128
Chapter 22 – The Early Years and All it Brings 131
Chapter 23 – So What Happens Now? 145
Chapter 24 – A Word in Closing 153

Chapter 1 - Introduction

Becoming a Mum has been the best thing that's happened to me... for most of the time.

Is it normal, I ask myself, to feel so much love for these two little people, but then at certain times feel so exhausted at hearing the sound of my own voice; I wanted to get them into bed ASAP? Yes - of course it's normal. But 5 pm is a tad *early,* love, string it out until 7 pm then *really* enjoy the peace and quiet!

I was and still am one of the lucky Mums who have several friends around me that I often use as a sounding board. I don't have the fear that I'm going to:

a) Offend them;
b) Bore them; or
c) Think they're going to threaten me with the authorities for being a rubbish parent.

I also, thankfully, have a supportive family network. Without these people, I would have thrown the towel in years ago.

I have asked myself: why did we do this? Why did we do this now? Why didn't we wait a few more years? But also: Why didn't we do this, years ago?!

So how did becoming a Mum affect me?

Well, lots of ups.

Lots of downs.

Lots of mood swings.

Lots of 'aarrrgghhhs!'

And plenty of 'why is that happening? Is that supposed to happen? And should I be worried about it??'

This book is NOT written to scare or glorify/exaggerate the experiences I had, but just to tell it how it was. And let you laugh with me (or AT me). Let me explain...

Chapter 2 – The Freedom

"Freedom….FREEDOM….FREEEEEE-DOM, you got to give for what you take!"

Ahh, the well-loved and missed George Michael often sang that to me through my old hi-fi system.

Looking back, I'd forgotten how much freedom we had when we didn't have to think about little ones. We could get up when we wanted, or not. We could eat healthily, or not. If we didn't go out all day, there was no one around to lecture us or jump up and down pulling at our legs to go to the park.

I've always liked children. As my Mum often liked to remind me, babies used to laugh at me. I'm not quite sure how to take that, but she did say at least they didn't all burst into tears. *Good point.*

I always wanted to hold babies and just gaze at the wonder of the little person two people had created. I always asked if I could hold a baby; I have seen some women (thankfully not strangers to the parents) just dive in and extract the child from the pushchair at lightning speed before the Mum could protest that she was just about to get little Harry off to sleep. At least I was polite.

Mummy-Friends were more than happy for me to hold their child, and some would just say 'hi, how are you? Hold Harry for a mo would you?'

'Er, sure, yes, no problem' I said, shoving the other half of my sandwich into my mouth. And off went said Mum, to get her well-needed coffee, child-free.

I'd thought about the day I'd become a Mum myself, thinking that we would decide to get pregnant when the time was right, and how our little family would grow. Aaahhh, how naïve I was! The reality of course was a bit of a shock.

Back then, I was still quite happy to hand the little lovelies back to their parents (especially following noises or, worse - went bright red, and was inevitably followed by a pungent smell). I liked the short-term loan basis, and I liked them 'smiley'.

My husband and I didn't rush at having children. We enjoyed living in our little flat. It was ok for the two of us – the lounge and bedrooms were fine in size, but the kitchen, however, was not. We couldn't both work in there at the same time – one of us would end up having a food-related accident, an elbow in the ribs, or a bruised foot.

We had a tiny mortgage at the time thanks to the state of the place when we bought it, so we thoroughly enjoyed spending our hard-earned money and savings *(savings? Oh yes, I remember those!)* on nice furniture, little luxuries (or 'tat' as my husband would call it), and generally enjoying our little nest.

I knew the flat was a great starting point on the property ladder, but 1 *really* wanted to expand to a house. Sensibly *(read 'very irritatingly')* my husband insisted we stayed in the flat as long as we could, as the house prices were on the rise. So, we saved our money.

We did have our little holidays though, nothing too flash - no Caribbean cruises or expensive flights; nor were the holidays the type whereby hiking up and down the land to see magnificent views were of top priority. No. We had lazy holidays. *Mainly* Spanish based resorts. *Mainly* because of a certain fussy eater. And that wasn't me.

We loved lounging by the pool. Yes, we chose the package holiday which included coach trips to see *those magnificent views*. You know – being driven up the side of a mountain or volcano in a vehicle that surely failed its MOT twice over, filled the beautiful cloud-free sky with plumes of black smoke as the driver revved the guts out of it to pull us up the mountain, and of course, felt like it was going to *tip over* the edge of said mountain or volcano at every turn. It was the 90's – when package deals were cheap and uncomplicated.

And of course, we always chose to go away *in school term time*. Wonder why that was...

At the time, we thought there was nothing worse than being in a lovely hotel, only to find a pool full of children splashing you, or worse – dive-bombing on top of you – on your so-called relaxing break. I feel bad just writing that now.

We always went for Self-Catering holidays, in little apartments, generally overlooking building sites, but on the odd occasion, we were lucky enough to get a glimpse of the sea.

We weren't lovers of camping. Actually - I hated it.

Now, I have my reasons. I like my creature comforts. I like the warmth of a *building*. I like being able to get up in the middle of the night to go to the bathroom, (which I always did – don't ask) which wasn't across the other side of a *field*. I like going to a bathroom in *bare feet*, rather than donning a pair of welly boots before my trip.

And I prefer not to be accompanied to the toilet, by any sort of wildlife, especially insects, thanks, and I don't want to hear any strange wild animal noises while I'm sat there trying to have a wee.

It's just me. Thankfully, my husband was on my wavelength too and wasn't bothered about camping.

Many have tried to persuade us otherwise and failed.

'Yes, we'll come and join you on the holiday. Tell us where the campsite is, and we'll book into the nearest B&B'. *No problem.*

Caravans *do* fall into the 'building' category, by the way, just to clarify.

So on returning from our annual lazy holiday, back at home, we ate what we wanted at all hours of the day and night, had the weekly trips across the road to the pub for the Sunday night quiz, then off to work on Monday and so the weeks went on.

Work for me meant Office jobs. I took pride in my work and enjoyed it. During the 90's I worked in a busy Telesales department for a then very successful magazine.

I was in my twenties and there was a huge social side to work. Every Friday lunchtime, half of the sales floor would go across the road to one of many pubs nearby, and then repeated the visit *again* after work.

'7 pm? Oh, I'd better make my way home now I suppose. Oh, hang on – husband has just walked in. Another round!

There was always a birthday/promotion/leaving do to celebrate, so going to the pub or a night out in town was a common occurrence. Drinking a frightening number of bottles of Hooch, Maddog 20/20, White Lightening cider, or whatever other colourful alcopops looked good on the shelf, on a Friday night, was the norm.

Not having children, pets or other commitments to worry about, and the body being young enough to cope with late nights and noisy pubs playing classic 90s dance music, why wouldn't you join in? It was great!

Of course, many of the people I worked with did have children. When new Mums came into work to show off their new arrivals, I was always one of the first to huddle round and coo over their new addition. However on one occasion, (I should say at this point in my defence I *was only 20* and a little naive about pregnancies), a colleague brought in her new baby to parade round, I stood over the pram, thinking how small the little bundle was.

'It's surprising how small he is considering how big you were…' I said, matter-of-factly, in front of most of the Telesales department.

What's everyone staring at me like that for? It's true. She WAS big when she was pregnant, and the baby was tiny!

I didn't understand why I was getting daggers from some, and others were too embarrassed to look at me…it was just an observation… Tut...

Children never really annoyed me, apart from the screaming ones in supermarkets that you just couldn't escape from. There I was doing the weekly shop, casually filling my trolley with all the usual 'treats', convenience foods, bottles of wine or a rainbow of those Alco-pops again, just taking my time minding my own business.

No distractions. Apart from that screaming child.

'Yet *another* mother who can't shut their child up', I'd think. 'Blimey, why can't you control your child?!'

'And what is a 2-year-old doing up at 9 o'clock at night anyway?? They should be in bed!!'

Hmmm – how your views change over time... well - some of them...

I was never confronted by any of those Mums, mainly because I just muttered it to myself under my breath. I dread to think what may have happened if I'd voiced my opinion.

So, our life was good and after a while of living together, we got married and had a lovely honeymoon...yep in a lovely hotel in Menorca – we splashed out and went half board that time!

At our wedding, we asked for no children to be in the church for the service, as we were worried there'd be some child screaming in the background all the way through and it would put us off.

Oh. My. God. Really??

Yes, I am aware now, that some parents would have taken their child OUT of the Church, had that happened, however, we'd had a recent experience of attending a ceremony for someone when they hadn't. The poor child could probably feel most of the congregation's glaring eyes on it, willing it to just BE QUIET!! The mother, oblivious to the noise of her child, continued wiping away tears of joy for the happy couple and was gently reassuring him that it was 'alllllll overrrrrrrr nowwwww'. Grrrr.

So that was our freedom. And we carried on as we were for another 3 years.

Chapter 3 – Married? Kids Yet?

As everyone who's ever been married will probably know, after a year or so, or sooner if they have pushy in-laws, the questions about children inevitably start. It wasn't a problem for us to make a joke and say 'yeah yeah we've got plenty of time' - we both wanted children, so the subject wasn't off-limits.

Our flat was spacious, but it had its' problems. We weren't sure when we were going to be able to move so we decided to start trying for a family anyway. But we didn't tell anyone.

So, my little dream of a family would begin – hurray!!

Only what started as 'yes we want children but are having fun practising', two years later we were still trying. It turned into a carefully planned, strategically documented, calendar-watching 'right the next 3 days are vital!'- mission.

It just wasn't happening.

I couldn't get pregnant according to my ideal 'when the time was right for us' theory. It was so frustrating, upsetting and certainly took the romance out of it.

I looked up all the things that are supposed to 'help' get us pregnant. Things like:

1) Knowing when you're ovulating: every day I would take my temperature and after a couple of months could see a pattern. The body temperature naturally increases when a woman

is ovulating. So, I had my little Excel chart (I know – sad), so we knew when the optimum time each month would be.

Oh, I could develop an Excel spreadsheet for *anything,* me.

2) The husband should wear loose boxer shorts instead of anything too tight. Done.
3) Taking a Folic Acid supplement. Yep, easy, done that too.
4) Sticking a pillow under your pelvis afterwards to help the 'swimmers'. Well if it's supposed to help, let's give it a try. Sexy, eh?

Ovulation Kits were available from pharmacists at that time, but they were extremely expensive. I certainly couldn't afford to do that month after month.

Still, nothing was happening.

But six months on, I couldn't believe it. We'd finally done it. That blue line as bright as day. So SO excited!! I was grinning ear to ear.

I'd had a few problems in the early weeks, but it all settled down and we had a scan and there it was - the little heartbeat. We told the Grandparents-to-be but no-one else at this stage as I was only about 7 weeks.

We excitedly and nervously attended the 12-week scan and planned to announce to all our news, afterwards.

However, to our shock and sadness, the scan showed that there was no heartbeat. Our baby had died.

We'd got used to calling it that, even just in those few weeks. I'd got used to saying I was pregnant, in my head. We were both excited about the months to come and suddenly it had come to an abrupt halt.

It's so hard to describe the feelings and emotions we both went through. We were so very upset, and it was horrible being led into a separate office to try and compose ourselves, so we could have a chat with the doctors, and discuss what would happen next. It was also horrible as we had to walk back out down the corridor, past all the people in the waiting room who hadn't had their scans yet.

I looked such a mess. They must have guessed what had happened, surely? I could feel the looks as I walked past. We were following another couple, but they were walking out grinning from their good news, chatting and hugging. I didn't know them, but I was jealous of their joy, angry that they dared to show it – just turn around and look at us!

I will never forget that day. It was a Friday. The hospital said that I would have to go home and either wait for nature to take its course and miscarry properly, which could end up being up to a couple of weeks, or, go back into hospital on Monday where they'd take care of everything instead.

There's no way I could just hang about waiting for it to happen, at any time - day or night, at home or horrifyingly, at work. We decided to go back in after the weekend. A weekend as you can imagine, wasn't great. I still felt pregnant. I still looked pregnant, as my stomach had swollen. How could this tiny baby inside me not be alive anymore?

We hadn't told anyone else at that stage, so I didn't have to go and tell people we'd lost the baby or face the embarrassing situation of people asking joyful questions. However, on that Friday night, we had agreed to babysit my Nephew. We couldn't let them down, so went round there, but they could see something wasn't right. Thankfully, they didn't ask. Just before they left for the evening, however, they asked us if we'd be Godparents.

So many emotions were then whizzing around my head: sadness, anger, bitterness, numbness, but I was also thrilled that they wanted us as Godparents, of course. But all I could manage was a smile and a thank you.

I think they were looking for a little bit more enthusiasm! But bearing in mind I'd been in tears all day, I struggled with the whole enthusiasm thing. Off they went for their evening out and I just sat crying on the sofa all night.

The following day when my husband broke the news of what had happened to the immediate family, they understood of course. And I also got told off for not telling them what had happened. But how could I? They were just on their way out for a good night out!

As the weeks went on, I found I wasn't dealing with the situation particularly well, and it felt like the whole world was against me. There seemed to be pregnant women *everywhere.* It was as if they all came out shopping at the same time to say, 'hey look we're having a baby!'

It was difficult at work too because, at the time, a colleague had just announced she was pregnant. I'd been off for a brief time and when I returned, although they all knew what had happened to me, it felt like she was almost flaunting it in front of me. As soon as I walked into the small department, they all started talking about how she was feeling, what things she'd bought, blah blah blah. I had moments where I just wanted to leap across the room like something out of a

Jackie Chan movie and shake her by the neck yelling 'it's not fair!!!' I didn't.

Paranoid? Probably. But at the time I couldn't help thinking about those things.

Two weeks after we lost the baby, I turned 30. It gave me something to look forward to – it was always going to be a good excuse to get lots of family and friends together in a hall, with good food and music, and the plan stayed the same, only that night, I got very drunk.

It was a great night. I vaguely remember…

We decided that we'd leave trying for a baby again, for a while, and concentrate on selling the flat, finding that little house I *really* wanted. We eventually found what we were after and bought a small place not too far away from both sets of parents.

We had lots of ideas of things we wanted to do to the house, not that it needed much doing to it, it was mainly cosmetic. The previous owners were obviously fans of Carol Smiley. Now I have nothing against her personally, but in the 90s, 'Changing Rooms' was certainly the thing to watch if you wanted a room – ruined. The programme consisted of people swapping houses with friends/family and decorating a room, with a team of 'designers' on hand to guide them into what would look great and 'freshen up' their friend's room. All done low budget. NOTHING compared to DIY SOS, I can tell you!

Yes, we watched as Carol and her team transformed a room from something relatively plain but *normal,* into a hideous mix of clashing fabrics and colours, patterns and ugly accessories. They could do a whole room in an hour, which back then, was (TV producers thought) a fantastic achievement.

Imagine samples of that programme in our house.

There were random blocks of colour in most rooms; for example, the small hallway had magnolia on one wall, and a big wall of pillar-box red on the other. Our main bedroom was Magnolia throughout, apart from the wooden concertina doors, which had been made for the built-in wardrobe, painted two-tone green, and not very well at that. And just for the finishing touch in that bedroom – the light switch – just a normal everyday white one – had a lovely green wooden small *picture frame* around it.

Wha……t?

The second bedroom was the previous owners' spare room. They'd gone to town on this, experimenting with designs. All the walls were white; the room had nice dark furniture in it when we looked around, however, they also had three 4-ft tall *trees* painted on one of the walls. Trees, which a 4-year old could have painted better. Just brown oblongs with green triangles on the top.

I kid you not. Oh, if only I'd taken a photo of these at the time!

I think we just stood there for a few moments in silence when we viewed the house, neither of us managed to say anything constructive.

I also hadn't realised it was quite popular to put leftover wooden laminate flooring from the lounge, into the upstairs bathroom for the floor. Oh, and for the bath panel too. Well, waste-not-want-not, I suppose! I want *not*, thanks.

We had plans to replace the kitchen pretty quickly. It wasn't particularly horrid, but it was grey, and the cupboards didn't close properly. So, we decided that this would be our top priority.

Oh, before I move on... how could I forget to mention the downstairs cloakroom! Stencilled French words in egg-shell blue on the walls and coat hooks that looked, well, like *penises* on the wall. Yes - that is correct. It was always a topic of conversation for anyone who came to our house. "Don't forget to use the downstairs loo before you go!"

However, within 3 months of moving in, we had to have a re-think about our plans.

Yep - I fell pregnant. Shocked wasn't the word.

Understandably, once we realised there was a baby on the way, those trees had to go. And quick!

Chapter 4 – Success!

I shall try not to be too graphic with the details of my pregnancies and births. There's nothing joyful about hearing how utterly *horrendous* a woman's pregnancy was or at the other end of the scale how wonderfully amazing it was, and how easy they found the whole experience! "Oh, it was a breeze!" It just ends up being a little…annoying.

It's the same with birth stories – why do some women feel the urge to explain *in detail*, and usually around a dinner table, the graphic details of their birthing 'journey' and how bad they had it? We all know one person like that.

I always feel sorry for the first-time Mum on the end of those stories, staring back at them in horror, their calm idyllic idea of how pregnancy and birth are, shattered.

Don't get me wrong, anyone who goes through hours/days of painful labour, giving birth *naturally* to a 10lb baby, deserves a medal (or a bottle of Prosecco all to themselves at the very least) for what they went through. But it's the ones who have 'been there, done it' and had everything ten times worse than you did, and then *brag* about it, that just annoy the hell out of people or is it me it just annoys??

These are also the very same people who, on pregnancy number 2, 3, 4, or more, compare their pregnancies, and then tell anyone who may have the misfortune to be in earshot, all about them too.

THEN they go on to give you a glowing report on how wonderful said child 1, 2 or 3 is now!

Let's get back on track again to the chapter in hand. So, there I was – 'late'.

I had all the same signs, but I'd forced myself to wait a good week before taking THE test. I know this may sound a little silly – putting myself through the 'am I or aren't I' stress for a week but I <u>had</u> to wait this time – just to be <u>100%</u> sure. There wasn't to be *any* cause for doubt.

The morning came and off I went into the bathroom. I came out, got back into bed and broke the news to my husband, who had his back to me at the time.

'It's positive' I said, grinning my head off.

He woke up quite quickly then and hugged me. Well, I suppose it was a bit early in the morning to expect him to be leaping about the room.

So that was that. Pregnant! The little blue cross was there as bright as day. No words saying 'Pregnant', no number of *weeks* displayed on it, no bells and whistles (I bet it won't be long before it flashes at you and plays Congratulations through a tiny speaker, mark my words). No, there was just a definite + sign.

We were elated, if a little nervous, because of the loss before. We both had a silly fixed grin on our faces and wondered how the hell we were going to keep it to ourselves for 3 months, especially as what waist I had, disappeared without a trace within a couple of weeks.

Oh, and I appeared to be very stand-off-ish with everyone. I think they initially thought I was just being unsociable. PMT lasting forever or something. But physically as well, I couldn't bare anyone coming within a few inches of me. Not because of the fear of being knocked or being accidentally elbowed as I reached for the biscuits at the back of the shelf at the supermarket, but for the fear that someone would brush against my boobs. Yes, they had inflated overnight and were very painful! And I mean VERY. God help anyone who attempted to hug me – aarrrghhh!

The Morning Sickness thing I was a bit anxious about but fortunately for me (AND my husband), I only had the continuous nauseous feeling and wasn't physically sick. It was still exhausting in the early weeks though. I was told that ginger biscuits helped with Morning Sickness. Anything which contained the word 'biscuit' in the sentence was bound to work, so I took that as *any* biscuit. For 3 months I got through packets of custard creams. Hey - no one questioned me (no one dared!). And I felt great eating them. And that's the most important thing….!

I did TRY the ginger biscuits. They did help. A bit. Well not much really.

We went for the 12-week scan and thankfully all was good. The relief you feel is indescribable, having had bad news before. We decided it was time to tell the Grandparents-to-be first.

It happened to be Mothers' Day that weekend coming, so we thought it would be a nice idea to surprise them and give the two Mums a little extra present - a small box with a baby's bootie in it. I know - I'd like to say I came up with that idea, but I didn't. Husband did well there.

My Mother-In-Law opened hers, grinned, then threw her arms around us both, and was relieved that FINALLY, her youngest Son was making her a

Grandmother. She was already a Grandmother twice over but couldn't wait for us to start 'producing' too.

My Mum, on the other hand, wasn't a Grandmother. Although I knew she was looking forward to us starting a family, she wasn't the stereotypical looking Granny. Not that she looked like something out of Dynasty either! (Sorry Mum – ahem). However, she always looked younger than her years, and there would be no argument that when the time came, she was NOT going to be 'Granny, Nanna or Grandmother'.

She had the little box and opened it. She looked a bit bemused, looked at me and then shrieked.

'What's this…? Wha… Are you…. Really??? Oh my God!'

She then burst into tears. Followed by my sister who was stood next to her. Then my Dad welled up. It was a lovely moment. So yes, she was going to be a Nannie.

Once we broke the news to other people, I ran out of fingers counting how many times 'Oh! New House – New Baby!' was shrieked at us.

Yeah yeah, of course. Want to fall pregnant? Just move house! 100% guaranteed. Hmm.

Chapter 5 – A Breeze!

So, the 9 months were not a 'breeze'. But one blessing was that I wasn't throwing up at every hour of the day and night. I do feel for those women who go through that. Horrible.

Normally I feel better after being physically sick. Yes, I know it's mainly been in the past due to *alcohol* but that's not the point. The point *is* that after being sick when you're pregnant, the feeling doesn't go away. For those Mums-to-be who get that all the way through – for months? My heart goes out to them.

I showed pretty much straight away. I had the 'thickening' of the waist – also known as 'STS - spare tyre syndrome' (Ok I may have just made that up) and all my clothes, already tight, would barely do up.

So, why wasn't my pregnancy a 'breeze'? Well, and I will keep this brief, it kind of went something like this:

Queasy; consistently high blood pressure; medication; weekly trips to the GP; chocolate; a 5-star holiday in Tenerife (we assumed it was going to be the last holiday we'd have for a while so hell why not stay in a good hotel!); frightening landing at Southampton airport on way home; hating the UK hot summer; more chocolate; 3½ Stone weight gain (something to do with the chocolate possibly?); eating copious amounts of marmite; an aversion to handling chicken fillets (the raw poultry type, not the things you put in a bra);

Antenatal Yoga (a funny experience); waters breaking; lots of giggling; pain.

Let's pause there for a moment… and take a break…

Chapter 6 – A Well Needed Holiday

A Holiday. Aaahh yes. Just the two of us. I remember it well! It was 2004 and we'd decided to go back to Tenerife and visit the places we'd previously seen back in 1991, the year we'd first met.

I was 16 weeks pregnant by this point and taking medication for my high Blood Pressure. The day before we were due to fly out, we had a check-up appointment at the Hospital, to see the Consultant.

Unfortunately, due to my Blood Pressure history which was diagnosed when I was in my 20s (I can categorically blame my Dad for that – it's hereditary for me), I was referred to Consultant Care for my pregnancy, quite early.

So, there we were in the waiting area at the Maternity Hospital. All sorts of people would come and go, from women hardly showing, clutching their partner's hand tightly, anxiously waiting to be seen to – let's say – a more *experienced* woman, with a brood of children running wild throwing themselves in the small ball-pit, causing mayhem.

Yes, you read correctly. There was a ball-pit, albeit a small one, in the waiting area of the Antenatal Unit.

For goodness sake...

Do you think it's a clever idea? To keep the kiddies occupied while their Mums wait patiently to be called?

In theory, yes. Practically, no. Balls get thrown out at everyone's heads, they're scattered around the floor ready for the unwitting midwives to trip over as they tried to get from one end of the unit to the other (sometimes that was quite amusing) and although it may be occupying the children, their shrieks of delight often turned into children kicking and yelling with despair when the Mum says it's time to leave.

In the Antenatal Unit, the clock never went as fast as it should have. They were *always* running late. I could never understand at the time how an appointment booked in for 9.15 am, could get so overrun that we weren't seen until 10.30 am!

We were called through to the Consultant area in threes, armed with our notes and the usual wee pot so they could test for all sorts. You start by shrouding said pot in tissues, burying it in your handbag, but by the nth time of being asked to bring one in with you or trying to wee on demand, the filled pot became an accessory walking down the road for all to see.

We then sat down and were called through to be weighed.

Just jump forward 6 months (go with me on this).

The whole weighing thing.

Or 'refusal to be weighed' thing, as a friend of mine had decided once.

Now I wouldn't have dreamed of doing this, as I was a scaredy-cat (some of those midwives and nurses were not to be argued with, just saying).

But there she was, my friend, at about 34 weeks pregnant, sitting alongside me waiting to be called in. When her name was called, she said:

'Actually, I don't really *want* to be weighed'.

'Erm, what do you mean?' said the nurse, clearly confused.

'Well, I wasn't weighed at the start of my pregnancy, so I don't see why I have to be weighed now – it won't mean anything'.

'So, you're refusing to be weighed then' said the nurse, quite indignantly.

'Er yes'.

So down she sat again and waited for the Consultant appointment. I looked at her trying not to smirk.

The next lady was then called.

'Actually, *I* don't know what I weighed at the start of my pregnancy, so *I* don't think I should be weighed either.'

Blimey, she's started something here...

I on the other hand didn't fancy arguing with the midwife in the weighing room, so just got on the scales. Then I too wished I'd protested!

Anyway, back to the 16-week check-up. We were called through to one of the little cubicles and there we waited - me on the bed and my husband by my side, waiting for the Consultant to come in.

Where is this Holiday I hear you ask?? Getting there, getting there...

At this appointment, in walked a rather tall chap, who we realized straight away, wasn't the Consultant; it was one of his Registrars. A common occurrence it would seem. We came to accept from then onwards that 'Consultant Care' usually meant 'Registrar-who-works-for-a-Consultant-and-hasn't-read-your-notes-properly-Care'. Especially when the first question was:

'And what tablets are you on?'

Really????

After filling him in, he read back through the notes, briefly, felt my tummy and agreed that I should continue to take the medication I had been prescribed. Ok – good so far.

'Do you have any questions?' he asked, totally without eye contact and completely expressionless.

'No, I don't think so... we're going on holiday tomorrow so I'm looking forward to the break' I said smiling, trying to at least get some sort of reaction.

'Where are you going?' he asked, still looking at his notes.

'Tenerife' I said.

'Flying?'

'Yes'...

'Oh no, you can't fly' he said very flatly, **still** looking at his notes. 'You need to be checked every week. Sorry, no. Ok?'

Then off he went!

My husband and I just sat there, in stunned silence. Then I promptly burst into tears.

Just before he was about to explode, the very nice Midwife we'd been having a laugh with beforehand, walked in and took one look at him, then me.

'Oh no,' she sighed, 'what's he said now?'

Does this a lot then, does he???

I couldn't string a sentence together, so my husband, quite calmly explained what he'd said.

'Would you like a second opinion?' she asked sympathetically.

'Shall I get the Consultant to come and see you?'

THAT WOULD MAKE A CHANGE! I felt like yelling.

'Yes please,' I sobbed, instead.

We didn't have to wait long and in walked the Consultant. A very nice chap with a *friendly* face. My husband was just about to launch into him about his Registrar when the Consultant very calmly said:

'So - you're off on holiday tomorrow then? Let's see... Mmm... ok. Have you got a blood pressure monitor at home? If not, get yourself to a chemist and buy one of the wrist monitors, they're not too expensive. Take your blood pressure every morning once you're up and about, preferably around the same time each day. Write the readings down. If it goes above this reading, take an additional tablet, if it drops down, go back to just one every day. Would that be ok?'

We looked at him, then at each other, relieved, but a bit lost for words.

'Erm, yes. Great. Thank you!'

'Now you go and relax and enjoy your holiday' he said smiling. Off he went.

And so off we went too.

The holiday was fabulous. We had a beautiful 5 Star hotel with an amazing pool, in a little up and coming place at the time called Costa Adeje, between Caleta and Las Americas in Tenerife.

The heat strangely didn't annoy me, as I thought it might. No - let's re-phrase that – the heat didn't annoy me *like everyone said it would*.

'Ooh going abroad when you're pregnant? Are you mad? Oh no, I couldn't stand the heat, me' said one.

'What will you do? You can't drink!'

Erm, try chilling out; relaxing; taking a stroll; eating; not having to go to work; more eating; having fun.

The only slightly annoying part, other than not drinking copious amounts of Baileys through a straw

(I got used to hearing 'a Jack Daniels and Coke please and a Diet Coke for the wife'), was that I couldn't lie on my front to get an even tan.

I still managed to go off-white though.

We got friendly with a couple, about the same age as us, at the bar – she worked in Public Relations, he was very vague about what he did, only disclosing that he worked in 'retail'. We ended up spending most evenings with them in the bar having very funny conversations. And yes, even though I was the sober one EVERY night, it didn't bother me. Yes, I was shocked at that too.

By the end of the holiday, we did find out why the chap was being a tad cagey about his job. After several drinks, he did admit that he was an Area Manager for Ann Summers.

'Why didn't you just tell us that?' we said laughing. 'What's wrong with that??'

'Well, you never know what reaction you're going to get from the women I tell. Some blush, some change the subject and try not to look embarrassed. The guys, however, tend to just smile in that 'God I envy you' kind of way, then get a dirty look from their Mrs and know they're going to be in trouble when they get home.'

We had great fun with our new 'holiday friends'. I say 'holiday friends', we did keep in touch for about 6 months after we returned home, but then like holiday romances, it fizzled out. Facebook was only in its early stages back then and we certainly weren't on it.

At the end of the holiday, I was 18 weeks pregnant and the blood pressure had remained stable. I had taken the readings as I was told and didn't have to alter the medication. So, to my Consultant's Registrar: ner-ner-ner-ner-ner.

My blood pressure was stable in Tenerife, as I said, until the flight home.

We'd flown out from Southampton Airport, which was surprisingly pleasant. Only 45 minutes up the motorway and at the time it was a relatively new terminal. I wasn't the best flyer, but as long as now and again I clocked the look of the air stewardess, I was fine. If she was calm – I was calm. Simple.

I did have to keep standing up as I was conscious of the risk of DVT in pregnancy, mainly because the health professionals kept *drumming* it into me, so I was wearing the very fetching black flight socks that the hospital had *insisted* I wear if I was going to go abroad.

Have you ever tried getting those things on?? You have to use ALL your strength to pull them on, and when you're pregnant, it's even more difficult, as you can't quite bend over properly!

I couldn't sit on the bed and do it myself, so in the end, I had to get my husband to help.

'Come on – lift your leg up a bit!' he ordered, laughing at me.

'I CAN'T!! I'll tell you what – I'll lay down on the bed with my leg out straight and you pull them on that way. This is ridiculous! How do they expect pregnant women to manage this on their own? AND you're going to have to do this again before we leave to come home again!'

'Ooh, the passion!!' he laughed.

I was not amused. 'STOP LAUGHING – IT'S NOT FUNNY!!'

Once they were on, my legs resembled a bit like a bone a dog would chew on – narrow in the middle and squishing out at both ends.

Attractive.

Once I was on the plane, I was advised to stand up regularly which unfortunately drew attention. I had some odd looks as if to say, 'what IS she doing?'

Once they saw the bump, I had the usual questions of 'when are you due? Are you ok? Aaahh, is this your first?', which, nice as that was in the first few months, after a while and certainly towards the end of the holiday, I felt like hanging a large sandwich board around my neck, and wandering around the poolside.

'Yes, I'm due in October; yes, I'm feeling ok thank you; yes, it is our first; and no, you cannot touch me!'

No one told me that when you're pregnant, there seems to be this untold open invitation for people to ask highly personal questions, or insist they touch your tummy, taking you by surprise all times of the day!

After our lovely holiday was over, we boarded the plane for our trip home, and we were sat in a row of three seats with a rather large middle-aged chap sat on the end of ours. I was next to the window with my husband in the middle.

As usual, I gripped his hand for dear life on take-off and once I was in the air, I was fine. Turbulence freaked me out, but I could see the wing, which hadn't fallen off, so we were fine...

The flight was also fine until we got nearer to Southampton Airport when we hit some major turbulence. It wasn't too bad initially, but it still made me feel uneasy. That, however, was nothing.

As we approached the Airport, the horizon out of the window seemed to be moving up and down quite drastically.

Ok - I know – it was the plane doing that, not the sky moving but I was irrational.

I then made the mistake of looking at the wing of the plane again. The plane was making my stomach churn. I can only describe it as being on a cross-channel ferry in very bad weather. You expect that movement on a ferry. Not on a plane.

The plane then dropped violently, and we braced ourselves for the landing. It was then that I grasped my husband's hand a bit harder than usual.

BANG. We landed on the ground with such force, that we thought the wheels were coming up through the floor! It was also at that point that the burly man sat on the end of the row, screamed out loudly in a high-pitched voice.

We both looked around at him and he was sat taking deep breaths and had his eyes shut. We faced forward again, hoping to come to a halt.

Please brakes work, please brakes work, please brakes work. Eventually, the plane slowed down and turned around.

We breathed a sigh of relief that we were down, were ok, and we just wanted to get off the plane and forget about it. Taxiing down the runway, we eventually came to a stop. We tried very hard not to get an attack of the giggles at our companion in the adjacent seat, poor man. He really ought to sort that scream out...

Once we were off the plane and back on the safety of land, we were met by my Dad who had come to pick us up. Now my Dad says things how they are and doesn't 'beat about the bush'. He'd watched our flight arrive.

'Bloody hell, that was a bit hairy, wasn't it? The plane was all over the place! '

'Thanks, Dad – you should've been where we were!'

According to Dad, we'd hit a crosswind.

Whatever.

All I know is that I haven't felt comfortable flying since.

Chapter 7 – Ballooning Nicely

With the Tenerife flight experience well and truly behind me, the months went on and I got bigger and bigger, not just the bump, but the whole of me. I looked like I'd been inflated.

I continued to attend the weekly midwife visits, where I was weighed, measured and plotted on the 'whale scale' as it was fondly referred to. The bump was growing nicely but was always on the bigger size, so week-after-week blood tests became part of the norm.

They always had a hard job taking blood from me, and I'm not the only one who has this problem, I know. You would think that they'd take notice of the patient sometimes; bearing in mind I'm the one who knows their arm better than they do, but no - they *always* tried taking blood from my right arm, even though I tried to explain that many have failed in the past.

But they knew best.

Oh look – the left arm works better! Told you so...

Unfortunately, one blood test showed up a high level of sugar and with the baby being on the big size, they thought I had developed Gestational Diabetes, something which usually disappears miraculously once the baby is born. This has to be monitored and controlled because if your body produces too much Glucose, which the baby needs to grow, the baby can grow larger than normal.

'This can make giving birth more difficult'.

State the obvious why don't you.

Now I've spoken to many pregnant women in the past who have had this diagnosed and found out that it can usually be kept under control by following a healthy diet and exercise programme.

Pardon??? But I'm *pregnant!!* This means I can eat what I like, when I like, in quantities I like. Doesn't it?

And *exercise???* I didn't do much exercise when I was 'without child'; I certainly didn't have any plans to start doing it when I was 'with' one.

Ok, don't panic, I thought, so my reading was high. They told me to come back after the weekend for a Glucose Tolerance Test.

Now what happens is, you're supposed to eat normally in the 3 days leading up to the test then not have anything to eat or drink apart from water, until after the test the next day.

'That's fine' I thought. 'I can do that.' Not sure how I'll manage without my cup of tea in the morning or more importantly my midnight snack, but hey it has to be done.

Eating normally for 3 days. Mmm. The thing that my husband once again pointed out *irritatingly* correctly, was that the doughnuts I'd been consuming leading up to the blood test showing high sugar, probably contributed to a high sugar reading. He said if I just lay off those, it'll probably come back to normal.

Now I *knew* he was right, but pregnant women don't need people to be right. They need to hear what they want to hear.

So instead I was just annoyed that he was right.

There was also the added issue of Chocolate. I just couldn't get enough of the stuff.

I was never one for eating loads of it before, but I certainly got the taste for it during. So, I laid off the stuff over that weekend too.

The three-day gap seemed like an age, to be honest. The more I couldn't have the naughty, sweet, devil food, the more I wanted it. But in I went for the test, praying it wouldn't come down to a strict diet or worse, injections.

The nurse took the initial blood test to check the level at the start, and then she disappeared. She came back a few minutes later and told me I would need to drink the sugary solution and have a blood test in 2 hours.

She gave me the solution and to be honest I struggled to drink it.

'God, it's quite thick isn't it?' I said, screwing my face up.

'Shhhhhiiiiii.......t' came the reply. 'Oh my God, I haven't diluted it. I am in so much trouble. She's gonna kill me over this. I could lose my job. I'm on my last warning'.

Er – never mind that - what may I ask is it doing to my body? Do I need to admit myself while I'm here?? I thought, selfishly and irrationally.

'Ok, ok' she was saying – I don't know if she was looking for input from me, or if she was just trying to calm herself down, but she was doing a lot of mumbling.

'Ok, it's fine, I just need to call the lab and let them know exactly what amount I've given you. They should be able to take that into account when they do the test'.

Looking back, she didn't seem quite 'with it' when she called me through – it was 8.30 am. Whatever the reason was, she managed to cover her tracks without it causing a detrimental effect on me or the test result. Or the baby for that matter.

Two hours later, after sitting in the waiting area doing <u>nothing,</u> apart from people watching, and that included watching several unruly children in that ball-pit again, I had another blood test, which came back... normal. Yippee!

Think I'll have a cup of tea. And a doughnut and bar of chocolate to celebrate...

They say you can start feeling your baby moving inside you from around 20 weeks. I was excitedly looking forward to this it was described to me as a 'butterfly' sensation. I got to 20 weeks and couldn't feel anything. A couple of weeks later and I still wasn't getting that feeling.

Being the calm, level-headed, non-paranoid Mum-to-be that I was, I mentioned this to my Midwife on our next appointment. Well, it was the *first* thing I mentioned as soon as I got through the door.

But she strapped me to the machine and there bold as brass was the heartbeat, beating away nicely. She explained that depending on how the baby was lying would depend on how quickly I'd feel it moving. But that it wouldn't be very long.

Of course, when the baby started kicking and moving around, I certainly knew about it as the weeks went on!

I found it fascinating. I would sit there of an evening 'playing' with the bump. Gently pressing on one side of me so that baby would move, and the bump would tighten up, absolutely solid. The shapes were amazing!

And in the bath! Such a lovely feeling, surrounded by warm water, almost weightless, and baby would start moving. I just loved watching it. But others weren't so sure.

Especially someone who hadn't had children. My sister, to be precise.

At 3 years younger than me, she lived at home with our Parents and enjoyed having cheap rent and a social life. But she was also really looking forward to becoming an Aunty. She just wasn't the broody maternal type at the time.

She would come over to ours and we'd chat about our week and how lucky I was that I wasn't still living at home… and how Mum was 'doing her head in' all the time…. And….and.

I'd sit there and umm and ahh at the right places, then all of a sudden jump as the baby moved. I'd then show her this obscene 'alien' movement. The bump was lop-sided and then baby moved back to the other side. It was so funny to see it! I loved it!

My Sister was a bit freaked out by it.

'Oh my God! That is *really* weird', she said turning her head away.

'Why? It doesn't hurt' I said. 'It's not going to all of a sudden explode out and grab you', I said, laughing at her.

'You're not seeing it from THIS angle!'

She was even a bit reluctant to feel baby after that for a while. Strange woman.

At 20 weeks, we also had a routine scan, and all was well. Back then we weren't asked if we wanted to know the sex of the baby – the hospital had adopted the policy of not telling you even if asked, but a year later they started offering that 'service'.

I wasn't convinced either way into thinking what we were having, so we decorated the nursery in neutral colours and bought everything as everyone does, which would suit both 'make and model'. There was a lot of Winnie The Pooh. Is that still the case?

The 2004 Summer was very hot, and although I worked in an air-conditioned office (something I now know to appreciate when you have it!), I was so uncomfortable.

I spent most of the time sat at my desk with my feet propped up on a box of paper, as my legs and ankles had swollen to gigantic proportions. No amount of water consumption was going to get them back to normal size, no matter *what* the Midwife said.

However, this ailment did get me out of running around. My colleagues helped me out and they didn't make me carry the hordes of coffee cups up to the kitchen for washing up. (We weren't important enough to have a dishwasher on our floor).

Also, at 7 months' pregnant I'd gotten so big that I had to swap cars. With my husband's car that is. I had a slight problem with getting behind the wheel of my little car. Some said I shouldn't have been driving, but the thought of giving up that little bit – no – big bit - of independence, was going to happen at the very last minute!

Chapter 8 - Worth a Try...

During that summer I'd decided, as it was my first baby, that I would try something my Midwife had suggested – Antenatal Yoga. My friend, also expecting at the same time as me, (the one who upset the hospital weighing nurse) had been going along for a few weeks and persuaded me to give it a go. So, I plucked up the courage – and energy - to go with her to the local class.

Well, what an experience that was. My friend had warned me:

a) The woman who ran it was in her mid-fifties, had white hair and spoke with a very soft voice (I guess someone with a booming voice just wouldn't have the desired effect) and that she was very 'new age';
b) Whatever I did – and this was VERY important - *do not* under any circumstances, make eye contact with her (my friend), otherwise we'd both dissolve into giggles and probably be chucked out; and
c) On practising the breathing techniques and various positions, you will get the urge to... fart. So, hold it in.

Ok then! No pressure.

She wasn't wrong. We all sat there in a circle on the chairs. One at a time we went around, introducing ourselves and stating how many weeks pregnant we were, and what we felt we would get out of the course. I'd never tried Yoga before, and the urge to burst out loud laughing was SO hard to control.

Amongst other things.

Looking around the group, there were various ages of ladies, most of us were looking uncomfortable and itching to learn how we could get a good night's sleep during pregnancy and also looking like we needed a good makeover.

Except for one lady, who always looked immaculate – hair and makeup perfect, and who - after a few weeks – we found out modelled swimwear in her spare time. I think it's quite fair to say that from the look of the rest of us there, we didn't model swimwear. No offence.

As the weeks went on, we got used to practising relaxing and the teacher would talk breathlessly in the background, coming out with all these Yoga terms, which were all new to me. Throughout the course, we practised various breathing, relaxing and birthing techniques, and we did get some good advice on how to make the day to day stresses easier to handle.

We practised birthing positions and what would be best for us on the day and we were reminded that we 'mustn't forget that we are in control and we should let the hospital know what we want to do, as it's our special moment and one to cherish'.

This class was held in a church hall, and there happened to be choir practice going on every week on the evening our Yoga class was taking place upstairs. Have you tried practising various positions with one leg in the air, panting, pausing, NOT farting, then hearing 'hallelujahs' from downstairs? It's not easy you know.

The other thing that the class was trying to promote, thanks to another expectant lady there, were organic services, such as Re-usable Nappies. This wasn't very common back then.

Now I was all for recycling *paper* and *cardboard* and taking my shopping bags to the supermarket, but I wanted our first experience of a baby to be as stress-free as possible. The thought of having to wash out nappies and dry them, as my Mum did 30 years before, didn't appeal to me very much. Just the thought now sends shivers. But each to their own and I know some of the group did try it.

I can't say it was my favourite of the Antenatal classes, but we did have some fun and the breathing and sleeping positions helped.

And it *was* very funny...

The actual official NHS Antenatal classes weren't so funny. They were more of a serious nature. My husband had agreed to come with me to one of the evening classes – sorry I mean THE one evening class they held that he could go to – as all the rest were during the day.

Once again, we were all sat round in a circle, at the local village hall. The Midwife and Health Visitor taking the class would talk about the basics; get you thinking that you really should breastfeed if you can, and how your partner can help you during labour. Some of the suggestions on that one were highly amusing.

Suggestions from the husbands/boyfriends such as calmly whispering that 'everything's fine, and it's all going to be ok', or mopping your brow, while you are trying to push a bowling ball out...

There was also the explanation of how giving birth was like pushing a baby's head through a square hole, then proceeding to pass around a doll poking out of a square hole in a cardboard box. Oh, it was very visual!

Then there was THAT Cervix diagram – a technical piece of equipment – passing around a bit of card which had a tab on it which you moved to show what 1 cm to 10 CMS dilation looks like.

Not many people studied this bit of the demonstration for very long, strangely enough.

C-Sections were mentioned briefly. And I mean *briefly*. Someone asked a question, which was dealt with by an official 'oh well hopefully you won't have to have one, but if you do, you won't be able to drive or vacuum for 5 weeks'.

That was that then.

A week before my due date, as another part of the Antenatal care, we had a tour of the Delivery Suite in the Hospital. On my tour, it was very quiet. Not much going on. So, it didn't have a lasting impression.

However, when my friend went for her tour, one particular lady was screaming her head off, much to the Midwife giving the tour's horror.

'Oh, it's not normally like this – there's no need for all the screaming – that's very dramatic'. Apparently when my friend was in labour, not only was she worried about everything else going on around her and pushing her baby out, but she was also trying very hard not to scream in case she'd get told off.

Chapter 9 – The Final Stretch

A month before my due date I had a scare where I had some bleeding. Not much, but I was told I had to stay overnight in Pre-Delivery at the Hospital for observation. It was very uncomfortable and very boring. Thankfully, it turned out to be nothing, but I still had to endure a night on the ward.

I was bored. Until a woman was placed in the bed next to me for the same reason – in for observation due to a scare. We got talking, got on really well, had a lot in common, and it made the whole 24 hours much more enjoyable!

In those 24 hours, we saw several ladies come and go, some were in short-term like we were, and some had been there for days. And some were waiting to be or had been induced as their impending new arrival, just wasn't making an appearance.

In particular, a woman was roaming the corridor, who looked like she was having triplets. She would walk the length of the ward then out through the corridor, umpteen times a day, to get to a certain fire escape to go outside for a cigarette. And *nothing* was going to persuade her not to go out; the Midwives had tried most methods they'd been trained in, and even the horror stories they were telling her, didn't stop her.

This woman had a look about her – don't get in my way, or else. What made her look even scarier was that she looked like she'd had an electric shock. She looked a right mess! Have some dignity please lady! We all know dignity is going out the window at the birth, but maybe she just thought oh what the hell.

We did laugh. And yes, I know, laughing at other people's expense is bad. But when all you've had to read was gossip magazines which you've read cover to cover, and can't get comfortable, people-watching is the next best thing.

And she was amusing. My new 'cell-mate' thought so too.

Five years later my companion in the hospital spotted me in a local park with the children and she remembered me from that stay. I'm rubbish with faces so was amazed she remembered me.

At 8 months' pregnant, I was sooooo uncomfortable. Rather than bite the bullet and go and buy a couple of summer maternity dresses and at least look bright and colourful, albeit rather huge, I opted for my more favoured 'comfort range' of jogging bottoms and T-shirt 'combo'. *Very* fetching.

I didn't care at the time, as long as I was cool (the temperature that is – there's no way you could interpret cool any differently at that point) and comfortable.

Of course, looking back at photos of my husband and me at a family BBQ we attended that month, wearing the said attire when everyone looked so lovely and summery and *feminine*… I didn't. It was hideous. I saw myself and thought 'good grief girl, what the hell did you look like?'

Sir Gok of the Wan would have been mortified. He'd have lifted them out of my wardrobe shouting 'What. The. Hell. Are. They???' and flown the jogging bottoms from a flagpole.

Throughout this pregnancy, but more so in the latter part of it, I also seemed obsessed with pregnant celebrities. Yes, I was a bit partial to a weekly gossip magazine, and one, in particular, I <u>needed</u> to get every week, just to see celebrities and their 'bumps' were doing. I would then sit there and, just to make myself feel even more depressed, *compare* my shapely (aka lumpy) pregnant figure, to theirs, look at how they dressed and how I wished I was more like them.

And of course, it made me feel a **whole** lot better. Not.

Two weeks before my due date, I started looking into all the things that would bring on labour. I just wanted the thing out of me!

One of the main things I'd heard about was Raspberry Leaf Tea. According to some beliefs, it contains vitamins and minerals that aid in delivery and bring on labour. So out I went and bought a large box of it.

Only it was foul. I just don't know how that stuff can be drunk! Each to their own I suppose, I wasn't one for drinking herbal drinks anyway. I think that was the problem. So, I managed to off-load it to someone else I knew was pregnant who rather liked it.

There was, of course, the usual list of things which I had read, that are supposed to help bring on labour:

- ❖ Eating a hot curry (couldn't face that);
- ❖ Going for a brisk walk (nothing brisk about waddling);
- ❖ Eating fresh pineapple (couldn't be bothered to prepare it – and according to experts - it *had* to be fresh);
- ❖ Excessive cleaning (certainly wasn't going to be this option); and/or
- ❖ Sex (nope).

When my due date arrived, I started getting excited and decided to leave the remedies for the time being to see what would happen. Any day now!

A couple of friends had already gone over their due date by nearly two weeks, however. 'Excited' wasn't exactly the word they used.

'Frustrating', preceded by a swear word, was described.

In fact, a friend of mine was still crawling around the floor 'den' building with chairs and duvets for her eldest, nearly two weeks over her due date with her second. I watched her and wondered where the hell she got her energy from.

'This isn't what I should be doing right now!' she yelled, rather peeved.

But you're doing such a great job and look at her face…awwww… I won't repeat what followed. Potty mouth!

Fortunately for me, it did happen quite quickly.

I was only a day overdue, bored and incredibly fidgety when I decided to start that 500-piece jigsaw (yes, I was THAT bored), that I had kept looking at for years on the shelf. My husband was debating whether he was to go off to his weekly ten-pin bowling match.

'If I don't go, nothing will happen. If I do go, your waters will break, I bet' he said, pondering on what to do.

'Well you might as well go; I'll call you if anything happens' I said, just dismissing the poor chap.

'Ok. I've got my phone but ONLY call me if something happens - ok?'

'Ok. Understood. Over and out. 'He looked at me and raised his eyebrow.

'Bye – take it easy!'

Off he went. It was 6.30 pm. Not hard to guess what's going to happen next…?

I was laying there on the sofa contemplating what packet to open from the cupboard next, and pushing the jigsaw aside when I shifted my hugeness over to reposition myself.

'Oooh I need a wee now' I said out loud to – nobody - and I stood up.

Then thought: actually - I can't control that!

Now let's just pause for a moment...

Ok. From what I'd seen on TV and found out in the Antenatal classes, they said that some waters break slowly and at the pace of a 'trickle'.

Some films/TV programmes show it happening with a little puddle, with the woman exclaiming 'Oh! My waters have broken!'

Surely not.

Others said it was like emptying a bucket of water.

Without being too graphic, I stood up and rushed to the downstairs loo, well, waddled quickly. I couldn't undo the damn knot on my comfy jogging bottoms, and no matter how frantically I tried, the knot wouldn't budge, so all I could do was just... well, sit down. Fully clothed. On the toilet. Giggling.

And it didn't stop. It was 6.45 pm.

I somehow grabbed a towel and the phone and rang my husband, who had just got to bowling and got himself a coffee.

'You are JOKING, aren't you??' he asked in disbelief, laughing.

I then dissolved into giggles again.

'Are you ok?' he asked, a little confused hearing all the giggling. 'Never mind, I'm on my way.' And home he came.

During all this giggling, I was wondering naively where all this pain was that I was supposed to *instantly* be experiencing when waters break?

I was led to believe, thanks to media, that you virtually collapse in agony the second it starts.

No. Again, not the case. What it does do, is lull you into a false sense of security, to thinking 'what's all the fuss about?'

We'd phoned the hospital and they said to come down to be assessed, so we gathered our stuff together and grabbed the hospital bag, which I had eventually packed the week before. I was still feeling perfectly fine, albeit a bit… soggy.

I had hoped that my waters had broken in somewhere like Marks & Spencer, as the rumour had it that if they do, you get a year's worth of shopping – bonus! I could live with that. But it wasn't to be. Maybe next time (next time...?)

My husband grabbed the nice new changing mat from the nursery together with another towel and placed it on the car seat for me to sit on.

Saves getting it valeted I suppose.

Another good idea from my husband – why didn't I think of that first?

And off we went to the hospital. It was now 7.30 pm.

Travelling down the road, quite calmly, we just kept looking at each other from time to time, grinning nervously. Oh, but then there it was – the pain!!

The pain my Mum once described as 'it's just like having bad period pains' she'd said, very matter-of-factly.

I don't know whether she was just trying to play it down to hide how bloody painful it *actually* was, or whether because the last time she had that sort of pain it was 30 years ago and she'd just forgotten, I'm not sure. Somehow, I don't think it's the latter, as it's something I don't think *I'll* ever forget in a hurry.

It *wasn't* like bad period pain.

The traffic lights seemed to be in our favour and although my husband wasn't hanging about, he wasn't driving like he was following an ambulance, we both wanted to get there in one piece. Thankfully, it was early evening, and the Hospital was only 15 minutes away. Well 10 minutes, that night.

We pulled up at the front of the hospital at the drop off point. I managed to get out and wander in, towel still strategically placed, leaving a few drips behind me, rather than a trail. I don't think anyone noticed…

Chapter 10 – Ok We're Ready... We Think

As I'd phoned ahead, and the midwife had agreed I could go down, I aimed for the Pre-Delivery suite upstairs, as instructed. There they assessed me and said that baby was definitely on its way. Unfortunately, due to the high blood pressure thing, I was immediately strapped to a machine and the contractions were happening quickly. My husband would watch the machine and warn me when one was coming - it showed up on the machine before I felt it!

So, all those positions I'd practised in Antenatal Yoga were a distant memory. I wasn't even allowed to sit up!

I'd been lying there for a couple of hours still in Pre-Delivery, and the contractions were so painful. Obvious question time - where was the pain relief??

'Oh no, there's no pain relief up here' explained a very *helpful* nurse. 'We'll get you downstairs as soon as we can'. And then off she hurried.

At that point, I could have jumped up and throttled her! Well ok, maybe after I unplugged myself first, rolled onto my side and with the aid of a winch to get me off the bed...

Another pause I feel is in order... for the Birthing Plan.

Now, I don't know about other expectant Mums, but the Antenatal 'chats' I had, and the many books I had read, all mentioned the Birthing Plan and the things you should consider, were listed something like this, and my answers were easy:

'Make sure you plan for the birth YOU want.'

'Write your Plan down – who you want with you in labour. Do you want this person to stay all the time or only for part of it?'

Only my husband there, please, and yes, all the way through; no, I don't want anyone else in the room. Certainly not my Mum or my sister. We're close, but some things I just couldn't have them watching. And I certainly don't want ANYONE in there with a video camera. Happy 18th Birthday darling – here's a film of your birth – enjoy!! And be scarred for life...

'State which positions you'd like to be in during labour and how active you want to be.'

Whichever position I can be in, depending on the pain at the time;

'State what pain relief you want to use and in what order.'

Gas and Air please, and if I'm not coping, an epidural as a last resort; I don't want Pethidine.

'Do you want to use a birthing pool?'

No thanks - can't be doing with all that. I'd rather be on dry land.

'If you have to have an Assisted Delivery, you may want to express a preference on the type of procedure.'

If I need assistance to give birth – do what you have to.

'Be clear about whether you want to breastfeed or bottle-feed the baby, or if it should have a mixture of the two.'

I will try breastfeeding first and see how it goes.

'Have your plan ready by 32 weeks so you know what you want.'

'Remember to pack the CDs too!'

Ok, so after quickly answering the questions in minutes, I then set about spending *hours* deciding what CDs to take into the hospital to have on in the background while I was in labour. Being a big music fan, I thoroughly enjoyed that bit.

WHAT????

What a waste of time THAT was. What was I thinking?? Whoever thought it would be a good idea to include 'choosing CDs' as part of the birthing plan needs their head examined.

My Birthing Plan - for a start - stayed in the bag, no-one asked me for it and because of everything going on, I hadn't remembered I'd packed one – it was the last thing on my mind.

And as things developed, I was in no position to dictate to them what I wanted. Unfortunately.

So, after two hours still stuck in Pre-Delivery strapped to a machine, I was eventually told I'd be taken downstairs to the Delivery Suite.

Finally! Pain relief was on its way! It'd better be good...

Along came a wheelchair to take me down. Once we got to the lifts, we waited.

A porter then came along to inform us that the lifts weren't working. They hadn't been working for about half an hour and no one had any idea when they were going to be fixed.

Wonderful. So, looking like I'd just run a marathon with a hairdo reminiscent of something an eighties revival would be proud of, I had to abandon the wheelchair and I had to try my very best to *casually* walk – or rather waddle and wobble - downstairs past various visitors, staff, and anxiously-waiting fathersto-be in reception, to the Delivery Suite. I knew people were looking but thankfully I had a dressing gown on over that horrendous back-side-flashing gown they'd given me, and I just tried to smile slightly as if everything was completely normal and this was my 'natural' look.

Once finally settled, I started on the Gas and Air and this was very effective, and I could even go so far as saying - I was enjoying it. But then that soon disappeared.

'It's not WORKING!!' I yelled at my husband.

I'd emptied the canister. So, he very quickly found someone to get a full one plugged in.

He was good at getting people to act quickly. He either used his charm or explained that he would be in a lot of trouble if he didn't come back and say, 'it's sorted'.

'It can't be empty' said the nurse, calling me a liar (little exaggeration there).

'It is – really' said my husband, laughing.

So, she put the full one on and off I went again. However, it just dragged on and on and the baby was just not budging. It had decided enough was enough and fancied a snooze.

If they want me – they're gonna have to come and get me!

I ended up having Pethidine – yes even though I said I wasn't going to - and after a few further problems, including a large red button being pulled resulting in a LOT of people rushing in, things calmed down and the doctors finally decided to get baby out by Caesarean Section.

My husband described that moment as one of the most frightening of his life.

The Doctors explained that I had to have a Spinal Block, in readiness for the operation.

A Spinal Block and an Epidural are not the same things, but I didn't know that. I didn't know what the difference was, and I was in no fit state to ask for details at that moment in time, so I just let them carry on. And I'm glad I did.

Epidural anaesthesia can be given at a point during labour which will block the pain from the pelvis and other areas. However, this can take up to 20 minutes to take effect, but a catheter is left in the back so that further medication can be administered if need be. However, because of the time it takes, some women are told that their labour is too far advanced at the point they ask for one.

A Spinal Block is also an anaesthetic, but it is administered with a smaller needle and without the catheter left in place and the pain relief is instantaneous and is used predominantly before C-Sections.

Well. Although uncomfortable having it done, it wasn't as excruciatingly painful as I had told myself it was going to be. When the medication started working, it felt so fantastic. The relief was indescribable. For the first time in hours, I was sat up and having a normal conversation, quite calmly, with all those around me. The woman, who gave me the injection, became the nicest person ever!

Once they were happy that everything was numb, I was wheeled rather swiftly into the theatre and my husband hurried into the side room to get into scrubs.

The atmosphere was tense but calm. That may sound a bit contradictory, but it was true. Everyone was moving around, each with their specific jobs to do, quickly but calmly. We were told what they were doing as they were doing it, putting our minds at ease, and ensuring they'd get baby out as soon as possible.

My husband was told to sit next to my shoulder and talk to me. However, he was being nosey peering over the screen watching the Surgeon with hands like shovels, dig in up to his elbows, and just after 1 am, out of the sunroof came a not-so-little 9lbs 9½oz baby boy!

So THAT was why he didn't want to come out! They said there was no way he would get through my pelvis and he was well and truly wedged in.

According to the midwife who took him, he was a 'lovely colour, not too mucky' and was making all the right sounds.

'He has an Apgar score of 10 – excellent' said the midwife.

'If you say so' said my dusband, a bit baffled. She beat me to it – I was going to ask what 'rating' they gave him – something I'd read in one of the booklets and fixated on, yet again. My husband didn't have a clue.

Should've read the leaflets then shouldn't you!

Not the right time for a domestic though.

I did manage to have a quick 'hello' with my new Son. However, due to further complications, I unfortunately then missed the next few hours after he was born, as I had to have a general anaesthetic once he was out. He and my husband were ushered out of Theatre so the professionals could finish the operation, and they had a bit of 'Father and Son' time together.

He helped weigh him in the old-style scales, ensuring there was time for the inaugural photo of the poor thing lying in a cold bowl, with everything in view to show the world his weight (and to bring out again on his 18th birthday of course).

He cleaned him up (yuk) and got him dressed, putting the standard-issue little blue knitted hat on him. And he sat and held him, while anxiously waiting for the doctors to come out and let him know that my operation was finished.

For the next three hours or so, I was watched over in the Recovery room. When I did eventually wake, I couldn't hold my son as I was too weak, and I certainly wasn't in any fit state to feed him. However, as he was still quite sleepy after his ordeal, that's exactly what he did for the next four hours – he slept.

This birth experience was one that my husband will NEVER forget. And I won't either.

Chapter 11 – Let's Do It Again!

I'm jumping ahead here I know, but it'll make sense later. Whilst we're on the Pregnancy subject, yes, we did it again!

Falling pregnant with child number two was a *totally* different experience to the first time around. We'd been told that no pregnancies are the same and no birth experiences are the same either. We thought we'd start trying for number two, knowing how long it took the first time, so we were relaxed and weren't in a hurry.

I'd contemplated getting the thermometer out again and resurrecting the excel spreadsheet which charted the temperature (I like to be organised – don't knock it) and even thought about spending the money on Ovulation kits, but instead, we just decided to see how it went first. I did start taking the Folic Acid again though.

You can imagine our total shock and disbelief then that after just two months of trying - wham! Pregnant. A pleasing shock, of course.

And the rollercoaster started all over again.

I waited a good week until I took the test and although pleased, I could tell my husband was a little apprehensive, to say the least.

As advised, I cut back on caffeine again (although I did have one large cup of instant caffeinated coffee a day, in the morning – I do need that 'kick' first thing!).

We waited until the 12 weeks scan this time before we told anyone, including Grandparents. We were celebrating my Dad's birthday and dropped it into the conversation that we were expecting again. Like you do.

I think the many questions asking why I wasn't drinking, was taking its toll on me, so we just announced and added to the celebrations.

A couple of weeks later, I was due to go out with my four close friends, for my birthday. It was always a drunken affair, and usually we arranged for a taxi or one of the husbands to go round picking everyone up and dropping us into Town.

I told everyone that my husband would be round to pick them up, however, they were rather surprised to see me driving instead. I blamed being on antibiotics for the reason I wasn't joining them in the drunken event – not very convincingly really – it was supposed to be my birthday meal out – we would normally have rearranged!

I picked up the first friend, who I could tell, was sceptical as to why I was driving. Once I'd picked up everyone, of course, I then told them.

'I knew it!' my friend said triumphantly. 'That was so obvious!' she laughed.

In this pregnancy, I told myself that I wouldn't put on another $3\frac{1}{2}$ stone, and as I was in a different job (I'd been made redundant when my eldest was a year old) it wasn't going to be as stressful either. The stress bit of that sentence was true…

So, this time it kind of went like this:

Queasy; blood pressure issues; chocolate (here we go again) – oh scrap that... bars of Double Deckers to be precise; a cold winter – brilliant - just covered up in plenty of layers; jogging bottoms yay; a sober Christmas (not so yay); and a girlie escape to Centerparcs at 8 months' pregnant.

This time around, I had a fantastic GP, who had been our family doctor for a couple for years up to that point. Unlike some GPs I've seen, this one took an interest in me and the family, enough to follow up on tests and be generally thorough and look out for me. He got my blood pressure under control from an early stage of that pregnancy.

My job at the time was also totally different from the last one. Previously I'd worked full-time in a busy department. This time around I was working as a part-time Office Manager in a more relaxed Government department, without all the stressful deadlines. Being the Care Industry too, it was very much about Work/Life Balance.

Plus it was 5 minutes from home and they operated a Flexi-Time scheme – perfect!! (If like me you get used to Flexi-Time, and then have to work somewhere that doesn't have it, it takes a bit of getting used to again. I MISS IT!)

My senior Managers in this job were really good too. Nothing seemed to be a problem. For starters, there was no clock watching; Antenatal classes took as long as they took, and there was no pressure to rush back to work for half an hour afterwards until your day officially finished.

One morning, I was struggling to feel enthusiastic about the day ahead and sat at my desk swinging around on my chair. At that point, my manager came around the corner.

'Sorry' I said, 'I just can't seem to get going this morning, I just feel like this baby is about to explode out of me'.

'Look, if you get up one morning and feel dreadful and can't come in, just ring us – we can manage, it's not a problem' she said, matter-of-factly.

I picked my jaw up off the floor.

'Thank you' I said, a bit surprised, 'that's kind of you'.

Well. That was a bit unexpected. I'd not been used to that.

There was one big downside to working in that office though – oh my God did they like to eat!

There were always endless boxes of chocolates, tins of biscuits or homemade cakes lined up in the kitchen. And my 'office' (aka a corner of the main office without a door) was *right* next to that kitchen. This was deadly.

I had NO willpower whatsoever and I think I ended up eating for four, not just for two. After giving birth the first time, I lost 2 of the 3½ stone I gained. Not bad. But by the end of this pregnancy, I'd put on ANOTHER 3 stone.

'Oh, I'll lose it' I said, stuffing my face with half a French stick filled with all sorts, from the mobile Sandwich Van. Yum!!

My Midwife at the surgery this time changed after a few weeks of me registering the pregnancy with them.

During an evening out with two friends of mine, when I was just over 3 months pregnant, one of them asked which surgery I registered at.

'Oh my God!' she exclaimed. 'I'll be your Midwife next month! I'm starting a placement there!'

Initially, we were both a bit 'is this going to be weird?', but when she confirmed it would just be check-ups and *external* examinations only, we breathed a sigh of relief. And this turned out to be great. I'd known her for about 15 years, but we didn't see each other very often. As I was on weekly check-ups again, we got to chat about how I was, listen for the heartbeat, etc, in between having a bit of a catch-up. I was also able to ask the silliest questions in the world and not feel awkward.

And just because you've had one child, doesn't mean you know everything when you have another one. For a start, you *forget*.

Don't deny it – you do *forget*.

And things change – especially about all the information on what you can and can't eat.

When I was pregnant the first time around, I read *everything*. I was very careful about the food thing. I had a strict list of things to avoid:

Raw seafood (including at the time – Prawns), undercooked meats, buffet food, unpasteurized cheeses, unpasteurized ice-cream (Mr Whippy machines), pre-prepared salads, Liver, Pate, raw eggs and foods containing mayonnaise; couldn't have 'runny' eggs, Peanuts; the list went on.

I was so desperate for soft ice cream during the hot summer in my first pregnancy that we'd heard that some places used pasteurised milk to make it, but they weren't very commonplace.

A couple of the restaurants we went to we had to check, as they used that sort of ice cream in their deserts and I couldn't have it, however, we found one!

A kiosk in town had both machines – pasteurised and unpasteurised.

That was the best ice cream I'd had I can tell you!

Four years down the line and second pregnancy – things had changed. Yes, some foods were still off-limits, but on discussing them with my friend – sorry Midwife – I mentioned prawns.

'Oh, you can eat prawns, as long as they're cooked properly, and you can eat peanuts, providing no-one in your family has an allergy. And pre-packed sealed salads are fine because they haven't been out exposed to the air and people touching them – unlike ones you make up yourself from a buffet-style deli. Mayonnaise was ok anyway, as long as it was a shop-bought one, not home-made. And you can have a runny fried egg, as long as the white's cooked. The shops use pasteurised eggs which are inoculated against Salmonella.'

Brilliant. So, was it *really* that strict *before?*

It's worth refreshing your memory second time around because the boundaries change constantly.

Alcohol was another hot topic of conversation.

How many times have you heard on the news one week it's safe for Mums-to-be to have a couple of glasses of wine a week, then the following week we're not supposed to have a drop as it could have serious implications. How can they keep changing their minds?

The older generation will tell you how it used to be safe enough to drink a pint of Guinness a week when they were pregnant, because of the Iron in it, or that they had two or three glasses of red wine a week and it never did *their* children any harm.

With both my pregnancies I did have a glass of red wine on the odd occasion, but on the second time around, I discovered a rather nice non-alcoholic lager, so went for that instead. It did feel like I was still drinking when we were on a night out.

I think this issue will continue to be discussed and the limits changed back and forth for many years.

This second pregnancy for me was also under 'Consultant Care' as expected, due to the Blood Pressure issue. I still had to go for the check-ups and sit in that waiting room for what seemed like hours.

Once again, I had tests galore and I did *try* to cut down on the sugary stuff. Thankfully, no sugar in the wee but yet again every time I was measured, the baby was on the larger size.

'You must just produce big babies!' the midwives would say.

The pregnancy thankfully went quite smoothly, until about 6 months when I developed Symphysis Pubic Dysfunction, or SPD, which is one of those pregnancy conditions which sounds a bit bizarre.

SPD means the ligaments that normally keep the pelvic bone aligned during pregnancy become too relaxed and stretchy. This causes some pretty horrid pain depending on the severity of it. It is also very common. But something I'd never heard of before. It certainly wasn't in any of the tons of leaflets I'd been given.

And unfortunately, you cannot take Ibuprofen or Aspirin when you're pregnant – they advise you to take just Paracetamol. But for muscle and joint pain like SPD, that didn't have any effect on me.

There are varying degrees of SPD - I didn't have it with my first, and why I got it with my second, is a question no one can answer. When they told me what it was, I was provided with a *lovely* elasticated pelvic support belt to use, which pulls the pelvic bones back into place. However, they're not very attractive and don't sit very well under trousers. Out came the jogging bottoms again! I also had a crutch for support which helped.

Along with this, you have to do some exercises and change the way you do certain things, like getting dressed sitting down, avoid lifting, that sort of thing.

Not easy with a 3-year-old to think about though. In the end, it was so painful, that I went to physiotherapy, especially for pregnant women with this issue.

Initially, I was very self-conscious being pulled about in my bra and knickers with this huge belly protruding, but the Physiotherapist was so lovely and was used to seeing all shapes and sizes, that she immediately put me at ease.

And wow it felt great afterwards. Phew - I could walk for a few days without pain. So, weekly appointments were a must.

SPD was one of those things that didn't get mentioned in any classes I attended so it was a bit of a shock as I had no idea what it was!

The Physiotherapist said that as soon as the baby was born, the pelvis would move back into its normal place and the pain would go almost instantly. I didn't believe her, but I smiled and pretended to be reassured.

She was 100% right though.

The weekly BP check-ups became tedious. But at least as the weeks went on, I didn't have to queue to announce my arrival at the doctors – I just held my arm up as I walked through the door, and the ladies behind the desk knew who I was, instantly. One of those ladies I became quite friendly with, which was very helpful when you're face to face with Mrs Frosty on reception. You usually have to go through an interrogation just to get an appointment.

Thankfully due to my GP getting my blood pressure under control early this time around and being in a completely different work environment than before, I was much more chilled.

Even with a 3-year-old in tow, it was less stressful. Because I worked part-time, I was still able to do the things I wanted to, however, I was exhausted by the end of each day. When you're pregnant with your first, if you're feeling a bit tired and fancy a sit-down, you can do just that. When you get in from work with a 7-month bump, with backache, and you want to flop for the evening – you can do just that. And if you have a partner that can, and will without bribery, run around after you too – you've got it made. You can put your PJs on and veg on the sofa.

Second time around – not a chance. You <u>have</u> to find the energy from somewhere to run your first to the childcare, get yourself to work, actually *do* some work (unless you know how to *look* like you're doing something, but aren't, because you're nearly asleep at your desk), pick them up again, get home, sort food out, get them to bed, and whatever other chores are facing you, *then* sit down.

No one tells you quite how different being pregnant is when you already have a child to deal with.

Of course, you also have to juggle all the appointments you have to attend, with a little one in tow too. And when they're weekly, it gets a bit of a logistical nightmare. And wasn't it typical? The Antenatal classes, Midwife surgeries at the doctors, and Consultant appointments at the hospital, all happened to be held on days I worked.

Thankfully as I said earlier, my employers were flexible and didn't mind when I had to go. I know other employers are not so accommodating and this adds to the stress of a Mum-to-be.

Chapter 12 – A Well *Deserved* Break

Just after Christmas in 2007, at nearly 8 months' pregnant with number 2, the five of us Mum friends of 3-year olds, decided to have a long weekend break at Centerparcs. I'd had my physiotherapy sessions leading up to it and it worked wonders –it got me walking and I was definitely ready for the break.

Off we went, leaving the husbands at home to deal with the children, while we relaxed and generally laughed for 4 days.

It was only an hour's drive away from home, and we'd seen the weather forecast for the area – it was January, so we knew it wasn't tee-shirt weather, however, we weren't expecting it to be as cold as it was. We took two cars. Three of us in one and two in the other.

As we approached the Parc, it started snowing. This could be interesting. I was nearly 8 months pregnant – I hadn't packed snow-wear, and my trainers were hopefully going to have to do if we walked anywhere.

With Centerparcs you can drive to your apartment/villa, unload all your stuff, then take the car back to the main car park, where it stays for the duration. Our villa, we discovered, was situated on the far side of the Parc. We arrived before the other party, so my two friends dropped me off with all the food and stuff and I said I would sort it all out while they took the car back.

I knew they could be a while, however, half an hour later it had started snowing quite heavily and they weren't back. It was also now dark, and they didn't know their way back to the villa very well. I was getting a little concerned.

Another 30 minutes later and my other two friends had then arrived and not having had any success in trying to get hold of the 'Explorers' by mobile, thanks to the RUBBISH network I was on, I asked them to try from their phone instead.

Someone picked up, but then after a strange noise, the phone went dead again.

Five minutes on and eventually we got through to them.

'Where are you?? You've been gone ages!'

'We're in the SPORTS BAR' she said, laughing. But before we could yell at her in envy and express how worried we were, she explained further.

It turned out that they were heading back to the villa when one of them suddenly slipped over. She was wearing her (fake) UGG boots, which were not made for snow or ice.

Rather than rushing to help her friend up, her companion just collapsed in laughter, and couldn't muster up the strength to pull her to her soggy feet.

At that point, the phone rang (that'll be us) and having eventually steadied herself to answer, she lost her footing and fell over again. It was the 'aarrrghhh' sound we heard on the line before her phone broke when she dropped it.

Having composed themselves, they managed to hobble to the Sports Bar nearby for a well-deserved glass or two of wine.

The remaining three of us unpacked the food and drink for the villa, although we'd brought enough to feed the whole of Centerparcs and waited for the injured party to return. Thankfully, it turned out to just be a twisted ankle, but still, we were hoping this wasn't the start of more mishaps!

Our accommodation was near the Spa area of the Parc – the main reason for us going in the first place. So, fortunately, we didn't have very far to walk. The rooms in the villa were split between the five of us and my friends were very good to me and gave me a room to myself with a double bed. Wise move.

Who wants to spend 3 nights in the same bed as an 8 month's pregnant whale?

One minute I was hot, then I was freezing, then I was up in the middle of the night because I couldn't get comfortable. They were just pleased they were in different rooms!

They were also pleased that I'd come along on this holiday, as it meant they had a good excuse to use the Land Train instead of walking everywhere, especially after too many glasses of wine, and of course, there was the snow to contend with. Not a good mix.

The Land Train was *extremely* handy. Although I had a job to climb up onto it, thanks to the additional *person* I was carrying. I relied upon having a bit of a push from the girls!

One of the gang also nearly fell out the back of it, as she forgot it only had plastic tarpaulin around it and not a solid side. Legs and arms flailing *everywhere.*

How I didn't go into labour from laughing at her, I will never know!

The weekend was fantastic. It certainly wasn't going to be one of those weekends where we'd have to get dressed up every night to go out, as that's not what the Parc is about, but after the events of only the first hour of being there, we decided we would stay in the villa that night and eat and drink and just chill.

Four of us took it upon ourselves to suggest that the fifth member of our party needed a make-over, so we set about planning this for the evening. We all thought this would be a great idea, and she didn't really protest, so we set about her doing hair and makeup.

Yes, these were the actions of a group of women in their 30s... helped along *slightly* by alcohol of course. You'd think the villa was housing a group of teenagers.

On Saturday morning, we woke up abruptly at 7 am. Not from any noise outside, however, but from a mobile phone.

It was one of the gang's Husbands.

She then proceeded to go into panic mode, wondering what on earth had happened for him to ring her at that hour of the day when she was away on a *relaxing* break.

Now I didn't physically *hear* the phone call, but from what I gathered once she had *calmed down*, it was something to do with a question about bottles for their 6-month-old daughter...

As you can imagine, she wasn't impressed. He on the other hand couldn't understand what the problem was ringing her at that time – after all, he'd been up since 5 am and was wide awake!

So, with our early rise, we sat about drinking coffee and chatting, enjoying our breakfast in our PJs, NOT having to think about anyone else other than ourselves. Bliss.

I can't tell you how much I was looking forward to the spa sessions we'd booked in advance. I knew I had to be careful with which spa rooms I went into as some aren't suitable when you're pregnant, but there are plenty which can be used, and I also booked myself a full body massage especially for pregnant ladies.

The massage was - fantastic. I was so relaxed, and they are trained to know exactly how to treat you and the bump and that hour was the best value for money I'd ever experienced.

After we'd been for our treatments, we stayed in our swimwear and complimentary dressing gowns and sat in the tranquil surroundings of the Aqua Sana, enjoying a drink and some lunch.

We then set about indulging ourselves in the luxurious surroundings of the Spa area.

However. One particular 'relaxing experience' wasn't so *relaxing* for me.

The five of us had been moving around in and out of the various Aromatherapy rooms, from a Finnish Sauna (too hot for me) to a Reflexology Footbath, or various worldly steam rooms. We'd got to the point where we wanted to just relax for a while on one of the loungers when we came across the quiet corner containing several comfortable chairs and water beds.

These were no ordinary water beds mind; these were *luxurious* water beds, surrounded by soothing music which would just send you off in a trance.

The girls got themselves comfortable and I had a bed all to myself. Again. Yet another blessing. I sat down on it, flopped back and chilled.

The bed wobbled quite forcefully when I got on, however it was so comfortable I just laid there. And I laid there.

Only I wasn't lying on my back, arms by my side, as the picture next to the bed shows. No. I had sat on the side of the bed and rolled onto it on my side. I then realised that I actually couldn't move. There was no way I could reposition myself – I couldn't get the momentum going to hoist myself into a different position like you can on a normal bed. So, I just laid there – trying to move, like a fish flapping about on dry land. Very undignified.

This was ok, I could just go to sleep anyway, and no-one was taking any notice of me. Then after about 15 minutes, the other girls decided to get up and move round to the next delightful experience.

One at a time they got up and gathered at the side, chatting away, and waited for me. Eventually one of them looked round to see me still laying there.

'We're moving around now, you coming?' one of them asked.

'Erm, any chance of a hand?' I said, trying to remain cool and calm.

But all I got in return were fits of laughter, which set *me* off and then I felt I was on the water rapids at a theme park.

Eventually, when they'd composed themselves, they gave me a hand to get up. Well two hands, they nearly did their backs in, in the process.

It's a good job I love 'em, isn't it??

We spent the remainder of the break, just wandering around the park. Although I couldn't walk too far in one go, we just made the excursions short and sweet, mainly going between the eating and drinking places.

We all had such a lovely time, and I didn't feel cheated about not being able to drink. It's the sort of group of friends every girl needs where you have can a laugh and chat about everything you want, without any limitations.

Chapter 13 – Been There Done That…

A phrase I *despise*… but the second time around, there was an element of that.

As you can imagine, even though they tell you no pregnancy or birth experiences are the same, trying to convince your other half that it would be a good idea to have another baby, was almost impossible, especially after the first experience.

When I did become pregnant, I spoke at length to my midwife about our concerns, as although we knew that C-Sections were more restrictive afterwards, we were worried about going through labour as we (sorry – I!) did before.

I'd also had conflicting reports that just because you had a C-Section the first time, didn't necessarily mean that you'd have one again, as they like to promote the 'natural' way. Of course, that opinion varied every time you mentioned it to someone different, but my Midwife reassured us that they wouldn't let us go through that again – that things would be different, and the Consultant would agree that I should have an 'Elective C-Section' at 39 weeks. Something, we were told after my Son was born. I wondered if they had referred to that birth at all.

As those weeks loomed, I was a little nervous that my body would go into natural labour, but the hospital assured us that if that happened, to give them a call and let them know that a planned C-Section was on the cards and I would be admitted in for the operation.

We got to 38 weeks and we were finally given our date to go in. They did warn us however that they had been turning people away at the *door* at that time unless it was an emergency, you couldn't come in – they were just too busy.

Can you imagine being that midwife or poor delegated person who has been given the task to turn these women away? Not a nice job. A pain-riddled, hormonal, ready-for-anything pregnant woman standing in front of you and you won't let her in?

'What the hell am I supposed to do – give birth in the car park??'

Good luck with that one!

I can now understand completely why people choose to have an Elective C-Section if they're fortunate enough to be given a choice of course. Or they pay for that choice. And it's got nothing to do with being 'too posh to push' I can assure you.

Unlike the first time, we'd planned the day meticulously.

Get up, get dressed, check the bag, which was packed nice and early, takes Son down to Nursery for the day, goes to the hospital, has a baby.

And it *was* that simple.

We were told to be at the hospital as close to 8 am as we could (my Son had a very early start at Nursery that day) and to make our way to Pre Delivery, where we sat in the waiting room. There were three of us ladies ready to burst, sat there with our respective other halves when a rather cheery midwife came in.

'Right, good morning Ladies and Gentlemen!' she boomed. 'The order of the day will be: You, You, then You' she said, pointing to us in turn.

Hoping and praying we wouldn't be last on the list - you risk having to be bumped to the next day if they get emergencies in – she pointed at us in second place.

'Ok? Good. If you would like to go through there and someone will be with you shortly' she said to the first rather nervous-looking couple.

'The rest of you take a seat in the Departure Lounge and you will be called through to get ready in turn. Thank you, people!' and off she hurried.

The rest of us sat there smiling at each other, commenting on how nice it was that not *everything* is serious in these places and some of the people are very nice.

About 10.30 am we were taken into a side room where I casually got ready into the gown. Husband and I sat there chatting on the edge of the bed. The baby was still kicking nicely.

When it was time, we walked, quite normally downstairs to the Delivery Suite. NOT looking like I'd run a marathon, NOT in pain, and my hair STILL looked tidy.

My husband was then taken to get into his scrubs. This time he was left to get ready at his own pace, rather than be dressed up like a shop mannequin quickly like before. When he returned, we both sat in Theatre, on the edge of the bed. Doctors and midwives were milling about, all very relaxed, laughing with each other.

'What shall we listen to this morning? Fancy a bit of Sheryl Crow?'

'What do you think Mrs Evans?'

'Sorry?' I asked. I wasn't paying much attention; I was too busy trying to get my head around how different it was from the first time – I was in the same Theatre as before.

'Oh, erm, yes why not?' I said, a bit baffled by it all. I wasn't going to risk upsetting the guy by slating his choice of music – I didn't know what part he was going play in the forthcoming event. And I did quite like a bit of Ms Crow at the time.

After a while, more people came into Theatre and there we were having a joke with the Anaesthetist and talking about everything other than what was just about to happen. Oh, and then I do remember being told that I really *must* lie still otherwise the spinal block wouldn't work if I kept moving.

Well, the Anaesthetist kept making me laugh! It was his fault...

So, after all the preparation, husband took his position, and the operation got underway. Again, intriguingly watching over the screen.

There was a lot of pulling this time, and I mean lots – yet again my small pelvis (still couldn't believe that fact knowing the amount of weight I was carrying!) meant the baby was stuck again...

It took a little longer this time, because of how the baby was lying and the two Doctors trying to deliver were 'pulling with all their might' according to my husband. To the point that he said the Doctor had her knee on the table trying to get it out!

But eventually, just before midday, out popped a once again not-so-little, 9lbs 5oz baby girl!

Having secretly hoped it was going to be a girl, I was just thrilled.

I had always answered the old question 'do you want a boy or girl' with the classic 'oh I don't mind, as long as it's healthy' line, but deep down I wanted a little girl and I couldn't wait to have some pink splashed about the house. My husband was pleased too, don't get me wrong, but he didn't have the desperation I did. I knew however that once our second was born, whether it was a boy or girl – that would be it – there would be no more. We weren't going to keep going until we got a girl. My body certainly wouldn't have been able to handle it!

Our new daughter however wasn't given the most elegant introduction to us. They didn't say 'Congratulations! You have a beautiful baby girl!'.

No. Instead they very blatantly *showed* us her gender!

'Ok. We have a girl!' my husband beamed.

'Yep it's a girl' the midwife confirmed.

'Are you sure?' I asked.

They laughed. I think they were qualified enough to tell the difference, don't you…?

She was placed straight on me once she'd been checked over and it felt amazing. The Doctors finished the operation, all went well this time, and my husband helped dress our Daughter, including the traditional pink woolly hat.

I was awake, I felt ok and I was thoroughly enjoying having that little face close to mine as we were wheeled out of the theatre and into Recovery. She just laid there with her eyes closed and all I could do was stare at her.

I didn't hear what Apgar score she was given, and it didn't occur to me to ask this time around…

I do think that for me, not having that same moment with my son after he was born, had a significant impact. I didn't feel that 'bond' with him as quickly as I did with my daughter. It came, don't get me wrong, but I did notice the difference.

It must therefore be heart-breaking for those parents who cannot hold and cuddle those tiny premature babies, and who have to stay in the hospital for weeks after they are born. I certainly feel for them.

Chapter 14 – Other Little Pregnancy Gems

Throughout both pregnancies, some other advantages and disadvantages should be acknowledged. Some of the lists can fall into both categories, depending on your situation – and also you can *turn* them into positives/negatives, depending on how devious you want to be!

- *Announcing you're pregnant:*
  Especially to loved ones. The look on their faces is priceless.

- *Food*:
  Pregnancy gave me a licence to eat and not be on a diet. Unfortunately for some Mums-to-be, the early stages are awful, and for some, they feel rotten all the way through, and the sickness is never-ending. For most, nausea does pass, and food becomes enjoyable again.

  However, with me, I think I took it to the extreme! I felt I could eat what I wanted when I wanted. No-one looked at me, judging what I was doing. I would just shovel that food in.

- *Heartburn:*
  A huge problem if you shovel food in! Oh, and it burnt. Of course, the more I ate, the bigger I got and the more heartburn I suffered from. I didn't have it before, which was a miracle

considering I was always (and still am) getting told off for eating too quickly, but it certainly raised its ugly head when I was pregnant. I got through endless packets of indigestion tablets.

- ❖ *Nosebleeds & Snoring:*

  Apparently, due to increased blood supply, some women can suffer from nosebleeds and start snoring due to the swelling of sinuses.

  Well, I did have the odd nosebleed during my first pregnancy, again, a bit odd I thought as I didn't generally suffer from them before.

  And I snored anyway I was told, so my husband didn't notice any difference. I'm sure I don't snore...

- ❖ *The Bump:*

  Having people compliment me on the Bump was quite nice.

  I'd have people offer me their seats in a variety of places, and people held doors open. Yes, this was all very nice. At first.

  By the end of the pregnancy, the novelty had worn off, to the point of snapping 'I'm fine, really!'

  Why did my Bump get so itchy?? What's all that about? I looked like I had fleas, the way I used to scratch at it. I had to use all sorts of creams and oils to try to make it stop – if you'd squeezed me, I would have shot across the room;

  People would stand in front of you, studying the Bump, and would even *walk around* you (self-conscious much?) and then say very

confidently 'oh yes you're *definitely* having a boy';

I can't see the Ultrasound machine strapped to your brain, so you know that - how...?

However, you can turn the size of your Bump into a positive – why not use it as a portable table while at a party/BBQ? When you sit down, you'll have two hands-free to be able to hold a drink in one hand AND eat with the other. Very useful. Oh, except when Bump tries to push the plate off. Be aware of that.

If you haven't felt the baby move for a few hours, poking the Bump and manipulating your tummy to get him to move – that for me worked well.

He/she's probably having a lovely sleep at the time, but hey, you're bored.

❖ *Stupid questions/comments*:
'Haven't you had that baby yet?'

Yes, I have, I'm just stuffing a pillow up into my top instead as I just want to *pretend* for a bit longer;

'Wide load coming through!' He got a slap for that;

'Are you sure you can't get out of the car? I left you loads of room your side.' Yes, if I was a size 6 then there's plenty of room. So, no – there isn't. Now move the car.

Being reminded of all the sleep you're never going to have again. 'Get all the sleep you can get while you're pregnant!'

Thanks, that's very helpful.

❖ *Talking to the Bump:*
You find yourself talking to the baby, which the professionals encourage, as they say, it gets baby used to hearing your voice. However, I'm sure they mean soothing things, not:
➢ Are you *ever* going to come out?!
➢ Stop dancing on my bladder!
➢ Why do you wake up for the evening when I'm just going to bed?
➢ Fed up now!!!!

❖ *Daily Chores:*
Aah yes. I'd like to say I didn't *milk* my pregnancies, but maybe I did an incy wincy bit.

But only when it came to washing and ironing!

Oh, and cooking dinner.

And washing-up. Have you tried to stand at the sink at 8 months pregnant with a huge bump?? It's VERY uncomfortable. You either have to bend double to do it or stand sideways. It's not good for your posture you know (lock that one in the memory bank).

❖ *Annoying people in Supermarkets*:
That's <u>them</u> being annoyed by <u>you</u> by the way. Waddling along, minding your own business, some people come up behind you huffing and puffing because you're not walking quickly enough.

A good tip: slow down even more and wander from left to right just for *extra effect*. You'll feel quite satisfied when you watch their body language once they've finally passed you.

- *Pregnancy Brain:*
    This is a genuine condition. Well, kind of. Not really.
    But it should be!
    The definition would be 'losing the ability to think sensibly and very often forgetting to do simple things'. Like walking to the top of the stairs, resulting in exhaustion, and then forgetting what you went up there for;
    Erm... I do that when I'm not pregnant too...
    Or coming out with some classic 'dim' comments, much to the amusement of others, embarrassing yourself in the process.
    You also feel the urge to talk about baby things at any given moment, then realising by the vacant look on their faces, that you're boring the pants off them.

- *Clothes:*
    You can wear the biggest, most unflattering clothes on the days where you really can't be bothered. AND you can go out of the house in them! No-one bats an eyelid because you're 'with child'.
    You can also convince your husband that you 'need' new clothes by wailing 'nothing fits, and I feel fat and frumpy!'
    'Ok darling, don't worry, here's £20.'
    Still sobbing: 'I'll need a little bit more than that, cos maternity clothes seem to be soooo much more expensive' (sniff).

- *Having to go to the toilet EVERY 5 MINUTES!*
  So annoying! Every restaurant. Every shop. Every park café.

  And having to get up to go 3 times in the night! You spend 15 minutes just getting into a position where you are finally comfortable, with your 3 pillows behind your head, and your L-shaped pillow sitting between the knees, a brilliant essential piece of equipment by the way - lovely, aah, sleep time.

  Nope. Your bladder then says, 'wake up!'

  So then my poor husband, who was now shoved so far over his side of the double (not King sized) bed that if he moved he'd fall out, now gets the feeling he's on a trampoline, as I manoeuvred myself to a position where I could roll up into a sitting position, then go off to the toilet. Again. In fact, with both pregnancies, my husband spent most of the time sleeping downstairs on the sofa, as I kept waking him up all the time.

- *Teeth, Hair & Nails:*
  On the downside, in both pregnancies, my teeth felt like they were going to fall out. No, I'm not making this up. This is a common ailment.

  But no-one told me that and I freaked out one morning and made an emergency appointment at the dentist. Unfortunately, this 'emergency' appointment couldn't be for a further 2 days. When I mentioned it at my midwife appointment in between, I got the 'Oh yes, that's very common. Nothing to worry about. You don't need to see a dentist'.

I sheepishly cancelled the dentist appointment...

On the plus side, my hair and nail condition were both amazing! I'm not saying it was like I'd just left the salon, waiting for a call from L'Oréal, but my hair was thick and shiny, and my nails grew like mad! Again, something very common in pregnancy and for once, very welcome.

❖ *Having a bath:*

Some ridiculous advice was given out years ago stating that pregnant women shouldn't have a bath, they should shower instead, as the heat around the tummy is not good for the baby.

The midwives thankfully confirmed this was rubbish and providing the water wasn't so hot you're left with red tide marks, it's fine.

Getting in is lovely. Easy.

Watching baby moving in your tummy while in the bath is lovely too.

However, getting out is another matter.

I managed to sit up, roll over onto all fours, and then eventually get to a standing position, praying the knees wouldn't give out. Then easy does it, and out you get. Not very elegant - but very effective.

❖ *Hormones:*

Ooh the big one.

This varies so much for pregnant women. Levels rise and then dip throughout the 9 months, but I had the usual extreme mood swings, where my husband could hardly say two words to me during the early weeks, in fear he'd have his head torn off.

But I had the horrible uncontrollable feeling of bursting into tears at the slightest thing, for most of both pregnancies. This was one of the worst side effects for me.

I'd cry over silly things, mainly things on the TV. It could've been anything remotely tinged with sadness and I'd be there with the box of tissues.

Or spilling the sugar over the floor, or anything dropped by accident.

Or if I saw anyone else crying, I knew that'd be it, I'd be in floods too.

And if my husband just had a funny expression on his face, I'd launch into the 'what's the matter with you? What have I done now? Why are you acting funny with me? I know I look hideous at the moment! I need a hug now!' stream of verbal rubbish.

However, at one point near the end of my first pregnancy, my husband thought I was going to go into labour while I was watching the comedian Lee Evans on the TV. I was crying so hard with laughter.

❖ *Old Wives' Tales*

There are so many old wives' tales to do with pregnancy, but these are a few of the ones I was told. I didn't necessarily *believe* them of course:

Boy or a Girl? So, you're carrying low…at the front…you're carrying a boy! Carrying high and all around, it's a girl! Then someone else will say it's the other way around. For me, it was the latter. All around – I had a boy, all out front, I had a girl.

The baby's heart rate is faster if it's a girl. Not true apparently.

Using a string, swing your wedding ring over your belly. If it swings back and forth, expect a girl; swinging in a circle promises a boy. The opposite is true (back and forth means a boy) if you hold a necklace over your hand.

So, the way you slightly move your hand yourself has nothing to do with it then, I thought sceptically...

Heartburn: If a pregnant woman experiences heartburn throughout the 9 months of pregnancy, she'll have a baby born with a full head of hair.

Well, yes, I did, and my two did have a lot of dark hair…

But apparently, they say that too if you eat lots of chocolate when pregnant. And I did that too, as we know.

Morning Sickness: if you had a smooth pregnancy with no morning sickness, it's a boy. If you were sick or felt sick during your pregnancy, it's a girl.

Well, I had nausea with both. I had a boy then a girl.

Hairy legs: Yes, apparently if the hair on your legs has been growing at record speed, you might be having a boy!

Really?? Well, I didn't look like I was wearing a gorilla costume at any time during my pregnancies, and still had a boy, soooo…..

- *Freebies:*

    Ooh, a good one! Initially, when you see the midwife, you get given your 'Welcome Pack'. Welcome to Pregnancy?!? Here's a load of information which you should read and digest, and tell your partner (because it's unlikely they're going to read it) and then place it in a folder keeping all your pregnancy literature safe and handy for when you need to refer to it.

    What happens is you go through each leaflet checking for 'money off' coupons, then think 'am I going to be interested in that? No. Into the bin, it goes.

    You can get all sorts of freebies though when you are pregnant from many high street shops; from nappies, wipes, to changing bags. Another good one is to register online for several pregnancy and baby websites and quite often they send things through to you as well.

    Another 'freebie' which I appreciated was free prescriptions. For someone on continual medication, this was much appreciated. AND free prescriptions continued for the first year of baby's life.

    Of course, when that had passed, I had to reluctantly start paying for them again. Grrrrrr…

- *And the main BIG plus while pregnant* – last but not at all least… drum roll, please… NO PERIODS!!! YAY!!!

    For someone like me who suffered for years with irregular, heavy, prolonged bouts of them, the 9-month holiday from them was a relief I can tell you.

Oh, and the 'no contraception' thing's quite good too!

Chapter 15 – Do This, Do That!

After both births, my husband had a comprehensive list of people I wanted him to call and text about our new arrivals and the order in which to call them.

My husband's Mum had said all along that as and when the time comes, we should call her as soon as we could, no matter what time of day or night.

The conversation with MY Parents before my first was born, was a funny conversation. We had asked them if they wanted ringing asap too, no matter what the time was.

My parents weren't Grandparents already. They were both still working at the time, and my Dad answered the question immediately.

'No, if we've got work the next day and it's in the early hours, leave it until the morning to ring us.'

I could tell by the look on her face that Mum didn't like that decision. But she didn't say anything.

'No problem' my husband said, not thinking much more about it.

Nearer my due date, Dad was asked the question again, just so that we understood – we didn't want to do the wrong thing at the crucial time.

This time Dad answered, pausing slightly, with a 'yeah, ring us whatever the time is'.

I wonder if Mum had had a quiet word...

When our son was born and everything had settled down, with both me and him fast asleep, my husband went and did the dutiful thing and woke the Parents at

2 am and told them the great news that they were Grandparents. I don't think they'd physically got to sleep anyway, as they were waiting for the call. They knew we were at the hospital, but I think they'd hoped it'd be a good 12 hours at least from when I went in, as that would've taken it to 7.30 am!

They were a bit shocked at the rude awakening at 2 am. And just to make sure the WHOLE house was going to know about the new arrival, my Mum then went and woke my Sister up, which must have taken some doing (she's usually comatose) to tell her the good news.

She didn't open her eyes – she just grunted, smiled, then went back to sleep.

My husband on the other hand, who hadn't had a good night's sleep the night before either, had at this point been awake for 24 hours. So, once I was back in the land of the living, and the sun was rising, he went on home. Unfortunately, he only managed to get another hour's sleep or so at home before he woke again, and then he started making calls to the rest of the people on the list.

He didn't take any notice of me when I said it's probably best to send text messages to most people. No. He decided to ring most of them instead and wondered why he spent so long on the phone that morning repeating the story over and over! He was excited and exhausted all at the same time.

He arrived back down the hospital about 10 am. And he did look shattered. But he was still smiling.

Of course, with baby number two, it was a civilised time of day. Grandparents were told and he called who he could, and he ended up leaving messages and texts as most people were at work. Do you see what I mean? Much easier to text people!

Chapter 16 – It's a Hospital, Not a Hotel!

My hospital stays were interesting, to say the least. I would like to start though by saying that the *majority* of the midwives I met, and there were quite a few of them, were fantastic. They had patience and empathy and they listened to me. And I know I couldn't do that job.

I saw a small number of women who didn't exactly warm to the midwives and gave them a lot of grief, mainly because of differences of opinion, on a variety of topics being discussed at their bedside.

One particular topic: feeding.

Mothers' views on how babies should be fed, varies from mum to mum, and this will never change. For some, breastfeeding is the most natural process, and both Mum and baby take to it like the proverbial 'duck to water', ending up breastfeeding for months and beyond.

Some try it for as long as they can, then for a variety of reasons they switch to formula milk.

For other Mums, they just cannot bear the very thought of breastfeeding and bottle-feed their little ones from the start.

Breastfeeding was heavily pushed in the antenatal classes I attended. They went into detail about the different positions you can feed the baby in; the technique; we had discussions about feeding in public places; how often you should feed the baby. We were advised that we should try as hard as we could to feed baby naturally – it would give them the best nutritional start and we should continue for as long as possible.

We all sat there listening carefully, wondering whether it was all going to go swimmingly for us. They then briefly mentioned Infant Formula. It is 'only a substitute for breast milk and should only really be used as a last resort' they said.

At which point my friend, there for the second time, just rolled her eyes.

I can't say I was overly enthusiastic about trying to breastfeed. Whether that stems from knowing I was bottle fed from the beginning because my Mum had problems, I don't know, but I was certainly apprehensive. My Mum was very good and didn't try and persuade me either way. She just said to do whatever was comfortable.

But I was certainly going to give it a try, and to be honest I wasn't *really* given a choice.

In the hospital, when it was finally time for me to feed my Son, the midwife came round.

'Right, are we going to give this a go then?' she asked in a rather commanding kind of way.

We?

Ok, just keep calm. You can do it.

But my son was having none of it. He wasn't fussed.

'He's not latching on yet – let's leave it and try again in a little while' said the midwife curtly and walked off.

Suits me, I thought. He wasn't screaming the place down, so maybe he just wasn't hungry.

A baby not latching on is very common and it takes time for both Mum and baby to get used to it. The other midwives I have to say were not so abrupt, and they spent time with me trying to get him sorted.

Eventually, he did latch on, but we had no idea if he was getting anything. And he was getting more and more unsettled.

When he was two days old, I developed a problem and had an infection in my milk and had to go for a chest X-Ray. Unfortunately for me, the X-Ray Department was in the main hospital, which was about a 5-minute walk across the main road.

Due to the operation and general anaesthetic, I still wasn't mobile enough to walk very well, and I just had this feeling they were going to ask me to do just that. And it also happened to be pouring with rain.

'Oh, don't worry, we'll get you some hospital transport' said the reassuring nurse sorting me out.

Relieved, I put on my dressing gown and fluffy new slippers and my husband sat me in a wheelchair and off we went to wait in Reception. And we waited.

Half an hour after they said I was ready to go across, I was still sat there. I was roasting hot, as the reception area was boiling, but I couldn't take off the dressing gown – I was still in one of the gowns they gave me when I went in... I'd have been rather *exposed* at the rear...

A taxi pulled up at the front. Yes, my 'hospital transport' turned out to be one of the local minicabs which we've all used to come home drunk in at one time or other. And it stank. It was still in the days when the Taxi Drivers didn't care about smoking in their cars – and this one certainly didn't care – it was horrid. But at least he didn't light up while I was in it.

It was only a few minutes' drive to the main hospital, but I felt worse just from that ride. The driver wasn't particularly helpful, so my husband went and got a wheelchair and helped me get in it. And off the taxi zoomed to his next fare.

I was wheeled through the X-Ray department, and everyone in the waiting area had a good look as I went past. Had I'd been more with it, I would've given them a nice wave as I jumped the queue, but I chose to keep my head down instead. In-patients take priority.

The X-Ray took minutes, as they do, and the nurses were mumbling behind the partition at whatever delights they could see on their screen. They didn't relay their conversation back to me, but it was done, and off I went back over to the Maternity Hospital in another taxi – a much *cleaner* taxi this time.

Due to some strong antibiotics, they said I needed, they advised that for the next day or so my Son should go on the bottle, but that I could try to breastfeed him again later that week.

Well, the poor lad was starving! They provided me with a couple of the pre-mixed bottles of formula which you just attach a teat to, and after emptying the first bottle, he then drank half of the second one.

He was a 9lb, 9½ oz baby, after all – he was a big lad!

I had been so stressed and in so much pain. My nipples were in a right state too, thanks to a certain little person's 'technique', so him feeding on the bottle meant I was finally relaxing, he was happy and the Midwives were happy too knowing he was getting some food (although I could hear one of the Senior Midwives sighing as she walked away on one of the occasions – yet another *failure* – yes I can read your mind missus!) I just poked my tongue out at her.

Once she'd walked away of course – I wasn't going to mess with *her*.

After four days of feeling like an inmate, I was climbing the walls. I'd been kept in that long because my blood pressure hadn't dropped sufficiently enough for them to let me go home. This was not surprising due to the lack of sleep and the fact they kept changing the blood pressure tablet each day, and to make matters worse, the Senior Midwife thought it would be a 'good idea' if I tried to breastfeed again, as apparently, I needed to kick-start the milk production again. I thought they'd forgotten about that...

I wasn't keen, but she was scary, and I found myself saying 'Ok' when I wasn't 100% sure. For the next 24 hours, I tried to feed but nothing was happening.

'Keep trying!!' she shrilled as she walked past.

'I. Am.' I said through gritted teeth.

That evening, my husband came in to visit, pulled back the curtain, looked at our previously very contented baby boy, now not-so contented, and saw me - a sobbing wreck.

'Right' he said 'this is ridiculous. Your blood pressure hasn't dropped, you're still on tablets, you've not had an ounce of sleep since you got here, and he's now yelling his head off!' he exclaimed pointing at our Son.

And off he walked at a marching pace. I was hoping he would find 'scary-midwife' and bring her down a peg or two; however, she wasn't around at that given moment. Then while he was off on his mission, a Junior Doctor appeared out of nowhere at the end of my bed.

'Good evening, how are you? Good.' She didn't take a breath and I hadn't answered.

She did the usual checks.

'I understand you've been for a chest X-Ray. Mmm...' she said listening to my chest. 'Has anyone ever mentioned a Heart Murmur to you before?'

'Er... No?!?'

'Ok, thank you.' And off they walked.

What the...??

Something else they want to throw in the mix?!?

But that was the only time anyone mentioned it, and I certainly wasn't going to either. So, I left it there.

I was sat there staring into space, tears streaming down, when my husband walked back in, with a rather younger, more attractive, midwife, who promptly sat on the end of my bed.

Why do they always find the pretty ones?

'Do you want to give him a bottle?' she said sympathetically, with her very non-scary face.

'Yes please,' I sobbed, rather uncontrollably.

And that was that. On the bottle, he stayed. He was born a big boy and continued to feed that way. In fact on the percentile chart which we grew to become obsessed with for some reason, he hovered around the 92nd percentile for his height and on the 75th percentile for his weight from the day he was born and is still that way now!

So, we were all much happier albeit still feeling a bit spaced out from the antibiotics.

That very non-scary midwife, who I happened to meet a year later at a girlie weekend away at Butlins (small World), showed such a kind act of compassion. For once she had the *Mother's* feelings in mind rather than just what the rule book says. When I met her again, I said where I knew her from. Her face was a picture. She looked a bit worried.

'Oh God – was I nice to you??'

I laughed as I explained the story. She was relieved and rather chuffed.

When I was in the hospital with my daughter, I was determined to give the whole Breastfeeding thing a go second time around.

Because my body hadn't gone through the whole labour thing, and only had the C-Section aftermath to deal with, I felt I was confident enough to give it a go.

My daughter got the hang of it quickly, which was great, but she was on me ALL the time. She <u>was</u> getting milk – not a great deal of it though, I wasn't producing gallons of the stuff; but she just wasn't happy unless she was on me.

I tried everything the midwives suggested, to help her and me. From changing positions to using 'nipple shields' – not the most attractive things, and they were a bit awkward, but they did give a bit of relief from the chewing (ouch!!); I tried a large selection of creams to use so I wasn't constantly wincing, but it was not the 'enjoyable' experience I'd heard it could be. They had observed and confirmed that she was obviously a 'sucky baby'.

I'd gathered.

After 3 days instead of 5 this time, I was allowed to go home. Once again, they'd messed up my blood pressure medication because the tablet I regularly took wasn't one they dispensed from the hospital pharmacist, so they 'made do'. It was up slightly but we mutually agreed that I would contact my GP when I got home to sort out getting it controlled properly again.

Once I was at home, I continued to feed her. I tried expressing, which did help although because I wasn't producing enough each time, it felt like if she was on me constantly. It was endless. And with a 3½-year-old to deal with too at home, I was shattered.

I managed this for a week.

'Not long enough', I hear some of you cry.

But I was quite pleased that I'd managed it for that long, bearing in mind the last time, but she was constantly hungry. Within an hour of feeding, she was screaming again, and my God could she scream, and I just sat there in pain from it all.

My GP was exceptional. I phoned him when we got home, and he came to see me.

He'd known us all for a couple of years and we went to see him rather than anyone else at the surgery. He was one of the younger doctors there with a young family himself and he was very straight-talking and didn't beat about the bush. He also had a sense of humour.

But on this occasion, he was NOT happy.

'Your blood pressure was perfectly controlled until you went in there' he said, clearly annoyed.

'Right let's get you sorted out.'

He came back every day during or sometimes after his surgery that week to take my blood pressure so that I didn't have to traipse up to see him each day, and he kept a close eye on me.

But at the end of the first week of being at home, it still wasn't as low as he'd like.

I felt the pressure from the Health Visitors who also visited in that first week, that I should persevere with the breastfeeding and I didn't want to give up.

But I was exhausted, she was hungry all the time, and my blood pressure was not healthy.

My GP sat and had a chat with both my husband and me.

'If you want me to make the decision *for* you, I will, on health grounds, because this is ridiculous. I'd advise you get baby on the bottle because it's clearly not doing you any good and I'm concerned about your blood pressure readings. She'll be fine on the Formula milk and you'll be able to see what she's getting too. And it will put your mind at rest'.

I was relieved. It was the right way to go. For my situation.

My daughter was finally contented on the formula milk, and within a few days, my blood pressure finally started to settle.

I look at Mums now that have continued to breastfeed their little ones for months on end and admire what they've done. I'm sure the professionals are still right that 'breast is best', but I don't think my children have 'suffered' because they were bottle-fed.

This is a subject which always has and always will be discussed for decades to come.

My stays in the hospital were experiences I certainly won't forget. I went home on the 5th day following my Son's birth. I thought I was going to be in there forever.

I was in a usual ward of four beds and saw a variety of Mums, some new to it all, some I could tell were definitely *not* new to it, as those were the ones visited by a fleet of their other children.

There were some very polite ladies in there – of course, I like to put myself in *that* category, who wouldn't, however, there were also some… downright rude 'ladies' there too, and God help if you got on the wrong side of *them*. They thought nothing of telling the unsuspecting midwife on duty that day or night *exactly* what they thought of it all – or them for that matter.

Visiting me on one occasion, my husband had seen three of these said 'ladies' standing at the entrance to the Maternity Hospital, chatting whilst they had escaped for a quick 'fag'.

All three of them were stood in their dressing gowns, wired up to a drip (not the same one of course – I know the hospitals are trying to cut costs but I think that would be going a *bit* far) and none of them had had the baby yet.

Not portraying the best image outside the main entrance of the Maternity Hospital, it had to be said.

Back on the ward, one lady in particular sticks in my memory. She had been brought in, in the early hours of the morning, and placed in the bay next to me.

Now being a first time Mum myself at the time, I had done a bit of research on the Internet (sometimes NOT the best option, as you often get a bit too much information) and I'd read books, and I did *listen* in the antenatal classes. So, I knew there were several things to check for if your baby is crying:

1) Is he hungry?
2) Is he too hot or too cold?
3) Does he need a change of nappy?
4) Or is he just lonely and fancies a cuddle?

However, the woman in the bay next to me didn't think of any of these things and would, throughout the day and ALL night, be the one pressing the buzzer to call for a midwife as the baby wouldn't stop crying.

Each time, a *very* patient midwife would come to her and try and help.

'Have you fed him? You need to try and feed him. Have you changed him?'

This woman (quite obviously to me!) wasn't trying these things and had to be told by all the various midwives who came on shift, what to do. Over and over again.

At one point, I felt like getting up, throwing back the curtains and saying 'Oh for God's sake woman, just feed it!!!' But I let the midwife who had eventually run out of patience with her, say that. Well, she was a bit more polite.

She was brought in on day 3 of my stay. That was the icing on the cake for me with everything else going on, and I was suffering from a severe lack of sleep. How the other women in the ward slept I will never know, unless of course, they had an endless supply of liquid Morphine (marvellous stuff for pain relief after a C-Section by the way!).

Not only was she pressing the buzzer constantly, but I was also kept awake by what she thought would keep her baby quiet: saying 'shush shush shush, shush shush shush, shush shush shush' constantly.

It didn't work and just annoyed the hell out of everyone else. Unsurprisingly...

In the end, on day 4, as part of his mission, my husband demanded that just for what would hopefully be my last night there, I should be moved to a side room if there was on, so I could get some sleep. They agreed. My son, who was sleeping very well throughout all of this, and once on the bottle slept for 4 hours between feeds in there, was fine! It was just me who had the problem.

That night in that side-room, it was so peaceful, and I did sleep. And by the end of the fifth day there, I was able to go home.

Thankfully when my Daughter was born, I went in on a Friday and came home on Monday. Apart from the hospital messing up my tablets, the stay wasn't too bad, and my companions on the ward were quiet souls!

Another learning curve we had to go through happened on day two of my first stay in hospital - we were told as it didn't look like I was going home anytime soon, we had to be shown how to bath our Son.

Now I was quite insulted by this at the time.

'Sorry – *learn* how to give a baby a bath? Seriously??'

Thankfully, my husband was with me when they suggested this, and just calmly agreed to be shown what to do. Because I wasn't walking very well and could only manage a few steps before breaking out into a sweat, I just sat in there while the practical lesson was taking place in the nursery part of the ward. The midwife then proceeded to show us both (mainly my husband) how to bath him without drowning him.

I wasn't paying much attention, to be honest, because when I say 'midwife', I use that term very loosely. She looked like Wurzel Gummidge in a nurse's uniform and I had to refrain from suggesting she took a bath herself.

Whilst you're washing his hair – here have some shampoo, love.

'Yeah; Mmm; Ok' I kept saying out loud. I think my eyes were shut though with my head resting on my hand. What I *wanted* to say was 'God I could do with a glass of wine and a good night's sleep'.

Thankfully, my husband *was* listening and seemed natural at bathing our son. And that became one of his roles once we were at home.

Remember that ladies – could be a good ploy to get the men to bath the baby more! So, all in all, although things didn't go quite according to plan and the first stay on the Post-Natal ward was quite eventful, I have to say that on the odd occasion that I did press the buzzer for help, all the midwives were very willing to help me – nothing was too much trouble, and I am very thankful for that.

Chapter 17 – Sshh –C-Section Secrets

The things I was worried about then, make me laugh now. Before I'd even had my first, I was worried about the birth and what would happen in labour. Especially the question: what if I tear?

Yes, I was fixated on this element of it, and was worried that this was going to be THE most painful part of it all - it frightened me to death!

As I've been through two very different C-Sections, I haven't had to experience the 'tearing' part of childbirth, thankfully. I have since been told by a friend who did go through it though, that you're so consumed with the contraction pains and people telling you one minute not to push, the next to keep pushing – *one more push!* - that you don't notice if you tear, and not everyone does of course. If you are one of the unfortunate ones, it's only *afterwards* that you know about it.

Something to do with stitches and weeing... say no more...

Of course, we members of the Caesarean club have other things to deal with. Things that, frustratingly, they *don't* tell you about before you have the operation.

1) Flab.
So, you've given birth to your beautiful baby. Those of you who are not over-weight and whose tummies shrink back to the way they were before (I'm not envious at all...), go with me on this. Once you've been

sewn up, you have, what can only be described as, this extra roll of flab hanging down, over where your scar from the operation is. You have to walk around holding said flab up off of the scar, otherwise, it can turn…technical word coming…manky.

I was extremely disappointed to learn after the op though that they hadn't respected my wishes – they hadn't done the tummy-tuck that I'd asked them to do.

I was serious! The Consultant didn't think I was, as he just smirked and carried on writing at the time. Tut!

So, after I'd had number two baby, this tummy seemed to hang over even lower, and I certainly had issues with it.

2) The Scar

They said that when they do the operation, they keep the scar discrete within the bikini line, and this is certainly true. However, the first one I had done, they secured the stitching at both ends with a small plastic ball. It was so uncomfortable!

I then found out after it went a bit 'funny' that the surgeon had done it up too tight. No wonder it hurt all the time!

'Wow, there's a lot of flesh to sew back together here ladies and gents – let's make sure it's well and truly on tight!'

Thankfully when I had the second C-Section, they weren't keen on using that type of fastener and used a different technique, more like a zip. I said I didn't care as long as it does the job and doesn't go a bit, well, yucky like before.

If you have to have a second C-Section, it's more than likely you will have a second scar, which would be slightly higher or lower than the first one. But of course, it depends on the surgeon. They say many women ask for the old scar to be opened up, so as not to have two to contend with. However, most surgeons like to steer clear of the first, as the healed tissue is best left alone.

And it'll be hidden, so who cares? These scars are not the type that you tend to flash around after a couple of drinks at a party.

'Hey, look at the scar I got – sliced my knee open ice-skating'.

'Oh, that's nothing, look at my scars – I've got two close together!'

Why has everyone left the room...?

3) You HAVE to get moving.

I know this sounds obvious. But I naively thought I'd be in bed after the operation, unable to move for at least a few days. While that was true to an extent, once you ARE up on your feet, and no longer having to go through the *rigorous* procedure of a bed bath (very rough – not impressed), you have to get yourself into the shower. This in itself is a huge energy-sucking event, and all you want to do is to lay still, coffin-like. But they keep on at you (something to do with 'hygiene', I don't know...) and so there you are sitting on the chair in the shower. A very handy thing to have there because the ability to stand for very long was slim to none.

You are also specifically told during this shower to 'hose' down the scar, to clean it. Then pat it dry with kitchen-roll type tissue (don't use ordinary tissues – they disintegrate and cause no end of problems!), and then you have to air it–'a bit like a delicate piece of fabric' the nurse told me.

Ok. What you, in reality, have to do is to *hoist* this spare tyre up with one hand, hose yourself down, dab very lightly (it's still very sore), get yourself dressed and then lie flat for about half an hour on the bed, still holding the spare tyre up and away from the scar area, so that it dries and gets 'aired'.

Yuk! This is a bit easier in hospital, as other than looking at your baby and sorting him out, you can just lie there.

However, try and continue to do this once you're home. It's uncomfortable, your knickers always manage to sit where the scar is, and the big knickers that they tell you to bring into hospital, *for* this reason, seem to have a mind of their own and roll down, ending up exactly where you don't want them to be, and it's not attractive at all.

And of course, there is the added complication that you can't just lie down for half-hour here, a half-hour there, at your leisure, just airing your bikini line for all to see.

You have a home to run and children to sort out too. Reality check!

Oh, the neighbours are coming over tonight to see our new addition to the family. Don't mind me, I'm just going to lay here and air my bits!

4) Restrictions

As I mentioned before, unfortunately, my Antenatal classes didn't give out a lot of information about C-Sections, only that if you are unfortunate enough to have one, you 'won't be able to drive for 5 weeks, don't do any vacuuming, and don't lift heavy things like washing baskets.'

Once you get home, it's quite shocking how much you *can't* do, without causing yourself pain.

Note: this is a good reason for not doing those horrible chores – milk it for as long as possible!

It does however depend on what your body has been through of course. I recovered much quicker after my second baby because my body hadn't gone through natural labour beforehand; neither did I have any complications.

But just the simple movement of bending over, turning around, climbing the stairs, pushing a pushchair, trying to lift an older sibling, or generally walking too far too soon, can cause so much pain.

Two weeks after my son was born, I thought it would be a good idea to go and show off my bouncing bruiser of a boy to my colleagues at work. At the time I worked at a Company that had open-plan offices, with loads of people crammed into it, on four floors of a building.

I'd worked there for years and the role I had meant I knew a lot of people. So, armed with husband and babe in a car seat, off we went to see everyone.

It was lovely. I'd not been out the house much in the first two weeks, so seeing everyone cheered me up no end. However, by the time we'd got to the fourth floor (don't worry, I wasn't silly – we used a lift), I'd come out in a full-blown sweat and had to sit down with a fan on me and a glass of water. I didn't look good. Not a good advert for having a baby!

I learnt a valuable lesson with our first – don't do too much too soon and DO accept help from others while you're healing.

Oh, one little but VERY important piece of advice to those of you who have had C-Sections: whatever you do – and I say this based completely on *experience* – DO NOT use ANY type of hair removal cream on or around the scar area.

It burns, and you have to get special treatment for it. And it hurts. A lot.

I very stupidly decided to use the said cream a few days before going away on a weekend break. Unfortunately, due to the dressings, I couldn't use the pool. It was so sore. I was so pissed off. And rather embarrassed.

Every time I see the product in the supermarket to this day, it makes me shiver.

Moving on…

Not driving for 5 weeks was <u>very</u> frustrating indeed, especially with my second, as I felt with her that I was ready to drive after 3 weeks. But I knew I had to wait. The reason they tell you not to drive is so as not to potentially do any further damage to the muscles, should the car have to stop suddenly. Also, should anything happen, the insurance could become invalid.

One of the issues I had to deal in the early months was that I had a bruiser of a Son. 9lbs 9½ozs at birth wasn't particularly small. So, trying to carry him about as he got heavier and heavier was quite a task in itself. But I think this may have helped build my tummy muscles up again!

Other than new Mums, no-one seems to like to talk about C-Sections. However, I did once get involved in a discussion at work about natural births versus them.

'Don't you feel you've missed out, not giving birth naturally?' I was asked at one point.

Yes – because that's what us women's sole aim in life is to do…

'Yes, I feel very guilty' I said sarcastically.

I've given birth, albeit not the 'natural way', to two beautiful healthy children, but I have not fulfilled my female role in life. So, I MUST continue until I can feel like a complete Woman! I felt like saying.

Of course, I don't feel I've somehow missed out. My body was put through quite enough throughout the two pregnancies and births, and according to several friends who have had babies the 'natural way', they said that a C-section might have been a better way, as my 'bits' are still intact and I don't have a dodgy Pelvic Floor! We'll leave that there, I think!

Chapter 18 – Reality Hits Home

You have all these ideas in your head when you're pregnant, about how it's going to be when the baby is born. I think I can categorically say that these go out of the window when the little one arrives.

I was quite spaced out on the antibiotics for the first two weeks of my Son's life and spent most of it in living in my pyjamas. We warned visitors of this <u>before</u> they arrived, especially as some people couldn't wait to descend on us the minute we got home. I didn't want gasps at the sight of me when they walked in.

I was tired - <u>all</u> the time. I know this is what you are told would happen, but you don't fully understand how tired you are until it happens. One guy I knew, who was not a morning person, used to get to work, slump at his desk and be grumpy for the rest of the day, complaining of having 'only 5 hours sleep'. He was only in his twenties and lived on his own.

What's that noise? Oh yes, the World's smallest violin!

'You're ok - you can catch up with your sleep tonight. I'd <u>love</u> to have 5 hours of undisturbed sleep a night, and on *consecutive* nights – that would be a bonus!'

Back to the early weeks, the routine was: *wake up, feed, change, wind (the baby, not me), cram in a quick shower – longing to relax in a bath for longer than 2 minutes; sitting and staring at baby sleeping for a bit;*

dozing off; waking up 5 minutes later, and so it goes on.

Oh, and of course, there's also keeping the house clean and tidy and sorting out the washing, ironing (a pet hate) and the weekly shopping.

Although, in the early weeks, I realised I had to rest, and I tried to do as little as possible. I was able to do this, thanks to my husband, who realised I struggled with things and it was going to be a slower recovery than I or he thought.

He learnt quite a bit during this period. He learnt where the Vacuum Cleaner lived. He learnt how the ironing board went up and down, and he learnt a lot about what you can and can't put together in a washing machine. He also learnt that the fairies don't come along and carry the clothes to the washing basket or indeed *put* the washing in the machine. They don't hang it all out on the washing line either. And they certainly don't get it in before the rain starts.

Ok, I think I can hear him now calling me a cheeky mare for that paragraph.

He did know how to do some of those things already. But still, I think his Mum felt a bit sorry for him having to do this because after he'd gone back to work, she then offered to do the washing and ironing for us in these early weeks. Initially, though, I was a bit reluctant.

'I'm sure we can manage' I said to my husband, indignantly.

'Look, she's offered, and this is to *help*, not to prove to anyone that you can't cope. It would help while you can't do lots of lifting.'

I gave in.

Thank goodness I gave in. It helped a huge amount – one less thing to think about. (Although I didn't send our 'smalls' round there... I drew a line at that).

But the best thing my husband learnt in the early weeks was how to bath, change and feed our Son. And he loved doing it.

He was put solely in charge of washing, sterilising, and making up the bottles. When I offered to take over once I was feeling more mobile, he declined my offer and continued to do it. I certainly wasn't going to argue, and he continued to do this until they were into 'Sippy cups' and also with our second arrival too!

I know I was *very* fortunate there.

Once my husband had gone back to work, my Mum came down and cleaned my house. She'd never offered before and hasn't since mind you, but I wasn't going to say no!

I was very grateful until I realised how long she was taking to clean it. She spent <u>ages</u> and she wasn't hanging about either! I started to feel a bit guilty and ended up apologising for the state of the house. The house which I thought was quite clean before she turned up and turns out there could be an improvement...

So, as well as dealing with all this tiredness, just for good measure paranoia set in - with vengeance.

Is he warm enough in bed?

Is he too cold?

Check the temperature on the monitor! Uh-oh, it's 23 degrees – we need to take layers off, open windows! Get it to 22 degrees!

The baby hasn't made a sound for over 5 minutes – I'll just go and check he's ok... Yep absolutely fine, looking as cute as ever, and <u>not</u> overheating.

How do people cope in hot countries? I'm sure they're not this paranoid.

I wasn't *as* bad with my Daughter; I did learn from this neuroticism.

Within the first couple of weeks of being at home with our new arrivals, I had several visits from the local Health Visitor, who explained that after having a C-Section, it was 'going to take time to heal and also for you to get your stamina back'.

You're not kidding!

However, she did point out that when I was driving again, that I should '*really* make an effort to come along to the local Under Ones group'.

Chapter 19 – Getting the Backside in Gear

The Under Ones group was held twice a month and would be a 'chance to get out and meet other new Mums going through the same experience as you'.

So, when my son was 5 weeks old, I rang my friend up who had also just had her baby – her second – and asked if she would go along with me, as I wasn't brave enough to go on my own. She wasn't going to go initially, but I twisted her arm by promising her a very large Gin & Tonic. She then agreed quite happily.

I didn't know what it was going to be like. I imagined walking into a room of women who all knew each other, the room going silent as I was looked up and down to see what kind of clothes I had on or what kind of designer pushchair I had.

What I was faced with was very different.

It turned out to the sanctuary I needed.

No-one noticed us walk into the hall, except for a woman on the far side of it, who at the time was trying to speak to a Mum over the noise of a yelling child. It was clear she was the lady running the group and she gave us a wave, then came over.

It was so noisy!

'Grab yourself a seat, put the baby down there and go and get yourself a tea or coffee if you want one, and you can go and weigh the baby over there. Lynn will help you and if you've got any questions about anything, just ask.'

So there we were, lots of Mums sat around the room, watching their little ones sitting in their car seats, or sitting upright on the mats, or crawling around chewing everything in sight, with lots of chatting, babies crying, and – shock horror – laughing!

My friend and I sat next to each other, chatting away, drinking our coffees and generally feeling a bit more alive than we had done over the past couple of weeks.

Around us were various types of Mums.

There were new Mums with babies only a few weeks old, like us, still, slightly shell shocked by the whole 'new baby' experience, and who just needed to be around other people in the same position. There were also Mums there who wanted to be heard and would tell anyone that listened about their experiences.

I'm glad I'd gone along with a friend; she'd been through this experience before, and chatting wasn't a problem - boy we know how to talk. So, we didn't have the issue of being too shy to talk to anyone else either.

We were sat with several girls who had plucked up the courage and gone there on their own and didn't know anyone else. We struck up a conversation and realised that we were all in the same boat – we all looked like we hadn't had any sleep since we'd given birth, all could have done with our roots doing, all sat there in our jogging bottoms or cheapy comfy elasticated waisted jeans – no designer-wear in-sight, and all sat there with babies who would at some point burst out crying.

Initially, my friend and I did wonder if we would keep going to this group, but as the weeks went on, we did go, and it turned out to be one of the best things we ever did. It was convenient, as you could get your baby weighed and measured and speak with the Nursery

Nurse there on a one-to-one basis, who could offer help and support and didn't speak to you in a patronising way. You could ask lots of questions – they didn't mind. Even when it came to things like... poo.

It's amazing how much interest you take in poo.

You study it; discuss its colour, consistency, volume, and how often they go; you worry about it if it looks a bit odd; you then discuss it further with other Mums at your weekly meet.

It's probably a good idea if you keep these sorts of conversations for these gatherings, but it is funny when you get odd looks from people or comments like 'oh lovely!' or 'do you mind?!' when you start talking about it at, say, work.

Mainly it's the childless men that can't handle it!

The 'Poo' category falls within those other 'don't dare to speak in public about them' subjects such as:

- Potty Training;
- Babies being sick;
- Winding;
- Breast Feeding (that should be top of the list actually!);
- Breast size or appearance after children;
- Leaking;
- Breast Pads;
- Chapped Nipples;
- Generally anything to do with the Breast area, unless of course, you're describing non-scarred, non-saggy, pert, perfectly formed page-3 girl-type boobs.
- But we Mums need to get these sorts of subjects off our chests (no pun intended) and the Under Ones group was the place to do it. We:

- ❖ Need to make sure our babies are 'normal' and are doing 'normal' things;
- ❖ Need to know that we're not worrying too much/too little; and
- ❖ Have to discuss these things to keep us sane!

There was always one person however at the Under Ones group. That one little 'ray of sunshine' that would be there from time to time just to have a good moan. And moan. And moan a little louder. And moan a little more if she needed more people to hear how horrendous her experience of childbirth was or how her child has had the worst case of *everything* that yours has had a mild case of, whether it be a common cold, cradle cap, nappy rash, colic; the list goes on.

And there was always someone there more neurotic than me. Which made me feel sooooo much better!

There were many activities that the Under Ones group provided as well as sitting around chatting. They would have speakers in to talk about issues close to our hearts; photographers; hand and footprints were taken; card making for Father's Day or Easter and even a visit from Father Christmas.

Under Ones was one of the best things I ever did with my first, because the group grew initially to about 8 of us all sitting together, and then we split in half and would regularly meet in our smaller groups each week, where we'd either go around each other's houses for coffee or lunch and have a good old chin-wag. Or we'd meet up for a walk somewhere; generally, anywhere which had a coffee shop.

It was rather amusing trying to get five of us plus pushchairs into the Café at Marks & Spencer. I don't think the other customers were too impressed. Tough!

We had the right to sit in there as well – we just took up a bit more room.

Another local meeting place for new Mums was the Doctors' Surgery, where every Wednesday you could take your baby to 'Weigh and Go'. It's a bit more than it sounds – you don't just plonk baby in one of those metal supermarket scales, weigh them then 'thank you – see you next week!'

But it's not far off that. You can also have a one-to-one with a Health Visitor if you have any concerns. This was very valuable and something I hope continues for the Mums in the community, as it is a much-needed service and free of course.

When I received my first visit at home from the Midwife/Health Visitor after I'd had the baby, I was given a red book which they use to record various bits of information about the child, from height and weight to immunisations, and it also has things in there for you to record, like for example, when they got their first tooth, or when they first stood up.

Every Wednesday, off I'd go with this little red book to plot my Son's weight and height on the graph and see what percentile he fell into to see whether my child was 'healthy'. Not that I had to fill the book in to confirm this, but it was another trip out of the house and I could see regularly how well he was doing...

I can't believe I actually did this until he was over a year old. I very rarely missed a week!

'Mmm, he's only put on an ounce since last week. Is that normal? Should I be worried? Should it be more?'

Get a grip love.

I was consumed by it. But I wasn't the only one. I'd see the same women week in and week out, all going through the same motions as me. That made me feel better, knowing I wasn't the only one.

And yes, you've guessed it: with my daughter, I didn't have *time* to go to the Under Ones for more than a few weeks and I *certainly* didn't have time to take her to be weighed and measured every week. She was lucky if got there every other month! Her little red book is quite empty compared to her Brother's.

Sitting at home in those early weeks, I started looking for other things I could do with my Son. Through the Under Ones group, a variety of leaflets were passed around about various other activities that were out there for Mums and babies/toddlers. I decided I would try something linked with the group and go to Baby Massage classes.

Now I'd spoken to several people about this who said that this was a lovely thing to do with your baby and was a free class that the Health Visitors ran.

So, my new formed friends and I decided to give it a go.

It was lovely and calm, you undressed your little one and laid them down on a soft towel, and then with some special massage oil for babies, you moved your hands over them in a certain way, to soothe and relax your baby. It was also apparently very good for babies who had digestion problems.

Unfortunately, *my* little one was having none of it. He cried, from the minute we got in there to the minute the class finished. Unfortunately having no clothes on was the main problem. For him. I was fully dressed, just saying.

I went back the following week – it was free, so I wasn't going to give up quickly – to see if he was having an 'off' week, however, he did *exactly* the same again. So, we decided to quit that particular activity and not disturb the babies who *were* enjoying it, any longer.

Trying to get to Under Ones or the Doctors' Surgery on time, however, was a Mission Impossible. Trying to be <u>anywhere</u> on time was a struggle. I hate being late for things, so I planned to give myself plenty of time before leaving the house.

No chance. *Oh, I've got an hour yet before I have to leave.*

That hour races by and then you're rushing to make sure you have everything in the Changing Bag – it's been checked twice already, but just in case the fairies come along and take something out when you walked into the kitchen, you check it again.

Then you realise the bib in the bag is dirty, so you go get another one.

Then you realise you've left the bottle in the flask on the side, keeping warm.

You also realise you haven't eaten yet today and wonder why you feel light-headed, so you grab a quick chewy bar to eat on the way.

Then you realise the baby has filled its nappy.

So after all that, you get out of the house, lock up, put the baby in the car, then realise you really <u>must</u> go to the toilet, as you'd been holding it for the last hour and your bladder isn't going to withstand any potholes in the road.

So, with a baby, it's just taken another half an hour to get out of the house!

Once I was back driving – freedom! It felt fantastic. With the first, I had all the time in the world to go where I wanted, when I wanted, without the pressure. I did a lot more walking with my first (like I said – all the time in the world) but after the second one, I needed the car – and quick.

We did make it easy on ourselves when it came to using the car. We had one of the four-wheeled Travel Systems. An easy to use car set which clips into a pushchair, which you can have facing you in the early months, and then once they're older they face away from you. Not so special you say.

No. BUT there is the matter of the fixed base. This does what it says on the tin. The base stays in the car, fixed in by the seat belt. You come along with baby already fastened in their car seat and with one click – it's safely secured in the base. Done. When it's time to get baby out of the car – release a button and there you go. So quick and easy and there's no fiddling trying to do up seat belts. The pushchair bit was also very quick to fold down, flat, into the boot of the car.

We had gone for the good old-fashioned four-wheeler, which wasn't 'on-trend' at the time. No. The thing to buy was a newly fashionable, more expensive 3-wheeler.

I didn't like the one I 'test-drove' in Mothercare. Nothing bad in particular, I just wasn't keen.

But my fellow new Mums were quite envious of my super-speedy folding/unfolding chair which slotted into the boot of my car easily. I was in the car and ready to go while one friend with her 3-wheeler was still trying to take the *wheel off* of it to get it into the boot of her car.

Chapter 20 – Second Time Differences

Before we move on, I want to look back on the two experiences, as I've noticed there were other things I dealt with quite differently, the second time around:

- *With the first*, you emphasize your bump as soon as you can and wear maternity clothes as soon as they start to fit.

    With the second, you squeeze into *normal* clothes for as long as possible or switch to anything elasticated, which will shrink back to its usual size afterwards.

- *Antenatal classes*: you go to all of them and practice all the breathing exercises, taking in all the information you can, with your first.

    With your second, you don't bother going at all because you haven't got time and because it didn't stop the pain anyway the first time around.

- *Baby Clothes*: with your first, you have fun buying all the little outfits and packs of bodysuits and arranging them neatly in your new cupboard in the new nursery, ready for the big day.

    With the second, you dig all those outfits out of the loft, wash them again, throw away any that have gone a funny colour or still have the faint horrible stains on, then pile them altogether in whatever cupboard space you have left.

- ❖ *Food*: you say to yourself over and over that you won't eat as much as you did the first time and that you're going to be careful.
    Then you're not.

- ❖ *Relaxation*: what's that? Any free time you had when you were pregnant with your first, like sitting with your swollen feet up for the WHOLE weekend if you wanted to, was a distant memory second time around.

- ❖ *Chores*: lifting and carrying all those things they tell you not to do, including lifting and carrying your first *child,* you ignore. And suffer the consequences in silence.

And once they're born, there were significant differences from having the first to having a second baby. For example:

- ❖ *Dummies:* I swore I'd <u>never</u> give a Dummy to my baby. I think that rubbed off from my Mum who refused to give me one when I was a child. She was quite adamant that I never had one. Until my Dad piped up in a conversation when I was pregnant with my first:
    'I gave her a dummy when you went out once'.
    Mum looked quite shocked. 'Did you?? I didn't think we had one in the house!'

'Oh yes we did' said Dad, confidently.

Mum wasn't impressed. Dad sniggered.

On advice from our Health Visitor, she suggested that to make our lives a little bit easier, we could give our son a dummy at night. So, we did. But only at night and he never went out of the house with it. I know! How many of you are rolling your eyes right now!

But common sense prevailed with our daughter: she had one from the start! Remember – she was a sucky baby? The dummy was *very* effective. Lesson learnt. Ok, it wasn't glued to her face all the time and certainly, she never had any *toys* swinging from it. Along with the dribble.

❖ *Sterilising & Clothes Washing: Everything* had to be sterilised, as they drummed into us, either in the electric Steriliser, or boiled to death. If anything fell on the floor it was put in the bag and taken home.

With number 2, bottles were still sterilised of course, but toys and dummies – not so much. If anything fell on the floor, give it a quick wipe off and pour a bit of water on it – done.

Same went for washing the baby clothes. I think I upset my Mother-in-Law once when she was very kindly doing some washing for us in the early weeks. She said 'oh it won't take long – let me do it for you. It's not that they dirty, I'll just do them on a quick 30°C wash'.

'Oh, you'll need to do them on a 60°C wash – otherwise, it won't kill the germs from the milk' I said, quoting the Health Visitor, and not thinking.

She just looked at me then changed the subject. Oops.

❖ *Dealing with crying:* With your first, there is so much going through your mind. All this information you've read/heard about and things you have to remember. The slightest cry and I found myself going to 'just check' they're ok and trying <u>not</u> to pick them up. Then *stupidly* picking them up.

With number 2, the baby is left to cry for longer, in hope that they settle themselves, which they can do, believe it or not! But you leave them just long enough so that they don't get too loud, otherwise, they'd wake up the other one sleeping in the next bedroom.

❖ *Weekly Activities:* Oh, the things I did with our first! Swimming lessons; hours of walking in the fresh air with the pushchair; going to the Under-One's Group; going to 'Tuneful Tots' (i.e. putting the child through a piano playing opera singer's class for babies and toddlers, with songs and instruments. Not one of my favourite classes I have to admit); watching baby playing, sleeping, breathing, just watching... And the favourite pastime with number 1 – alternately going round one of the girls' houses every week for lunch and a chat.

Things I did with number 2 – taking number 1 child to his swimming lesson; attempting to go for a walk to the shops with eldest in tow, which inevitably ended up going back for the car to get us there quicker; attending the Under Ones group once a month if lucky; going to the Supermarket; watching baby number 2 sleeping? Didn't happen. Watching baby number 2 playing – a little, but mainly watching that child number 1 wasn't poking, hitting or 'cuddling' number 2 too hard! Going round the girls' houses for lunch had stopped due to work commitments for them, so those of us who managed to get a day off a week tried to grab a coffee together when we could.

- ❖ *Work:* I was very lucky when I had my first, in that we'd planned for me to take a year off work on Maternity Leave. Unfortunately, at the end of that year, I was made redundant. It took another 3 months before I got a job, so I'd had 15 months off with him.

    With my second, I could only afford to have 8 months off at the most from work, however, again, I was made redundant from that job (never getting pregnant again if I want to *remain* in a job – there was a pattern forming!). I desperately wanted to have more time off with her, however, it wasn't to be.

Chapter 21 – Something's Weighing Heavily

I'd been trying to diet since about 1998. It may seem a bit odd to you that I can remember the year, but I remember it well. My weight had gradually been creeping up since the early '90s for no particular reason, other than poor eating and not enough exercise, and I have battled with it ever since.

Back in 1991, when I was in my late teens, I was very slim and could eat anything I wanted. But something happened in the few years following this, not sure what, and that wasn't the case anymore.

I yearned to be back at that sort of weight, but I've accepted now, that is NOT going to happen!

My problem is not medical – it's psychological. I love food. I eat most things, but the problem is first - the portion sizes; and second, I eat for comfort and boredom. And given the choice, I would live on bread *all day long*.

I'd joined a gym to try and shift it – I've joined the same gym mind you about 5 times since the mid-nineties. As many people find in life, situations change and the gym became a chore and together with not eating very well, the weight slowly increased year on year.

In 1998 we set a date for our wedding for the following year, so I was on a mission to lose some weight. I joined a weight-loss group and did the old 'sitting in a circle and clapping all the weight losses and getting the 'head tilt to the side' look together with a 'had a little gain this week' comment when I'd had a bad week.

Once I was married, my weight gradually increased. Then with the weight gain of both pregnancies, in 2008 I was the biggest I had been – EVER.

I always said, 'I'll worry about the weight after the birth', so mentally I wasn't willing to try and I always had an excuse. But that year I was in panic mode.

Three months after my daughter was born, I was in the local supermarket and bumped into someone I'd seen while I was pregnant some months before.

'Oh, you must be due any day, now mustn't you?'

'I've had my baby' I said, flatly.

'Oh yes! Yes of course you have – I knew that. Sorry!'

She looked embarrassed.

I wasn't impressed. We chatted for about another minute, and then off I went down the next aisle. She also went off... my Christmas card list.

Six months after my daughter was born, I had to return to work. However, having been made redundant, I had the horrid task of firstly finding a job and secondly, impressing them.

With no clothes to wear.

As nothing fitted. Not even close.

I couldn't squeeze into anything, as any slight movement and I could have burst out from God knows where.

I ended up going for interviews in Maternity trousers, pulled in around the waist. Well, I don't think they would've been too impressed with me if I'd turned up in my trusted old jogging bottoms.

I got myself a little part-time job, and the hours suited both parties.

I just went in, did my job and went home, nothing too stressful or tiring, just right. So, time to concentrate on losing some of that weight.

I decided to go on a particular very low-calorie diet and over the next year, I lost just over 4 stone.

I will always battle with my weight and since that time I've gained quite a bit – not all of it, but more than I'd have liked!

I did feel fantastic at losing all that weight. However, there was also a downside... not only did I have stretch marks from having the children, but I also had stretch marks from losing weight! My body looked like it needed a good iron. Not a good look for someone my age.

They say that stretch marks can be a hereditary thing. Again, I refer to 'Sir' Gok of the Wan, when he says, 'you have to accept that they're part of <u>you</u>'. And unless you have tons of cash to spend on getting rid of them, you're stuck with them.

Although I was back to the weight I was 10 years before, my body was a completely different shape.

'That's what having a child does for you' said one 'expert'.

Thanks for that.

My boobs had lost their shape and had to be hoisted up daily so they're not keeping my waist company; and my waist still had the fold of skin there from the C-Section, reminiscent of a deflated rubber ring, which gets much bigger if I eat too many sandwiches.

High-waisted Jeans are now the only rail I look at, and my ARM would fit inside Skinny Jeans, but not my legs!

Chapter 22 – The Early Years and All it Brings

So, there we have it. Two children, one of each. No-one can explain the unconditional love between you and your children.

I have certainly become more protective as you would expect, of my family. I was never one to get into arguments with strangers or even friends for that matter, but God help anyone who moaned that I was in the way with a pushchair!

And there are lots of those people about, unfortunately. I'm sorry, but I'm NOT going to leave my baby in the pushchair near the entrance to the shop, just because it's taking up room in the queue that I'm in, so *stop tutting*!

Sometimes I was just in the mood for someone to voice their opinion – 'go on just say it, *I dare you!'* I thought to myself when I'd been up for most of the night before.

Ok, so maybe five of us all with travel systems trying to work our way through that M&S cafe, may have been a bit annoying to those whose chair I nudged into (not *barged* into as one man exclaimed) but we had to put them somewhere...

I'd always been an organised person: it was one of my skills and all my jobs have required me to apply that skill.

I thought I could be as organised at home when it came to children.

So so SO not the case.

It was like I'd turned into a different person!

Clutter and clothes were everywhere. When I tried to tidy up and thought 'ah that looks better', I came across another sleepsuit under the cushion or bib down the side of the sofa.

The one main thing you noticed as you walked into my lounge within the first year of having a baby wasn't the nice ornament on the shelf or the new clock on the wall, but the pile of nappies, wipes and changing mat that had found its new home in the corner of the room.

And of course, the box of toys strewn over the carpet; the bouncy chair; and play-gym which no amount of tidying would hide.

Our lounge wasn't 'our lounge' anymore.

And that was how it was and would be for years to come. Something we and others who came to our house, accepted.

We didn't have a big house; we didn't have a separate playroom to store toys. At Christmas and on birthdays, the lounge looked like a ran-sacked aisle in Toys-R-Us. When anyone came in the door, we gave them a Government Health Warning that ankles could be broken if they didn't look where they were going. *We had to cover ourselves, you understand.*

Getting organised to leave the house, did improve the more I did it. Sometimes if I knew I didn't have to be anywhere, in particular, that day, I'd time it so that I could go into town and do a bit of window shopping and get some fresh air.

These types of excursions were fine. Apart from a Changing Bag and maybe a bottle keeping warm in a flask, there were no major hazards in the way.

Arranging to start taking the baby to 'Mother and Toddler Swimming' was a completely different kettle of fish.

The girls had been talking at one weekly catch-up, and someone (I can't remember who, but will never forgive them) thought it would be a good idea if we took all the children, who were about 6 months old at the time, to the swimming pool for the Mother and Toddler class, to get the children used to swimming.

The girls thought it was a fantastic idea. I on the other hand was filled with dread. I could see a couple of issues with this *fantastic* idea.

a) I'd have to get into a swimming costume. I hadn't worn one for a VERY long time. In fact, I dug it out of the drawer under the bed which never gets opened (because you can't get access to it), and the fabric lining of the costume, crumbled. *And* it had somehow shrunk in that drawer...; and

b) I would *really* have to organise myself to make sure I remembered to take everything AND get there on time.

So, the day arrived, and I had organised a costume, shampoo and a towel for me. Easy. Mind you, after a few weeks this ended up just being a costume and a towel, as there was no way I could fathom out how to get a shower and a hair-wash once we'd got out of the pool, with a baby in tow.

For the baby, I had to make sure I had a towel, a Swim-Nappy, swimming trunks, nappy sacks, wipes, nappies, and a spare change of clothes for any 'accidents'. All to be taken into the changing room in the over-bulging bags.

Once we'd found our little corner of the bench in the ever-so-crowded changing room, I had to make a decision: who do I get undressed and ready first? Baby? Yep – not a quick job, especially if you have a dirty nappy to contend with too, but fine. I can handle that. But then, what do I do with *him* while I get undressed? Put him back into the car seat? There's not enough room in the changing room for car seats – there were Mums and kids everywhere, with stuff scattered all over the place.

I know - I'll put him into the playpen provided, then fight with the locker, then pick him up. By now, he's crying as he didn't like being dumped in there for all of 2 minutes. Not a good start – we hadn't even got into the pool!

When we finally got in it, he loved it. We had lots of bobbing up and down, lifting them in off the side, splashing around, all to nursery rhymes. Brilliant. It was only half an hour but fortunately, my son was one of those who loved the water and I enjoyed it too!

Then it was time to get out. Sigh. Ok deep breath.

We'd taken the towels onto the poolside for the children, so we wrapped them up and got back into the changing room. I managed, whilst holding him, to get the stuff out of the locker and thought it was more important to get him warm and dry first.

I on the other hand just froze.

But that was how it was going to be if I was going to continue to take him to this class. I couldn't give it up just because I couldn't *organise myself* properly! All the other Mums managed it, and they didn't look particularly stressed. Well a couple of them did...

Eventually, it got a bit easier, especially when they were sitting up on their own and I could let go of him whilst I got dressed.

One advantage of having the children in the car – being able to legitimately use the Parent & Child parking bays, especially at supermarkets. I wasn't the sort of person who, before children, would just park in the family spaces for the hell of it, but oh my word – there are plenty of people who do. And it's one of my bugbears now. My local store hasn't introduced parking fines yet for those who use Parent & Child spaces 'irresponsibly' as they do in some areas of the country – maybe they should.

I'd drive into the car park of my usual superstore and eyeball other cars making their way towards the Parent & Child bays, really wanting to put my foot down and get there first, but I refrain and keep it calm. The relief if there's a space or a spot someone is about to reverse out of! Is that sad or am I not alone in feeling that way?

But of course, some don't care about where they park. The elderly (Ok, I don't get too wound up about them using them); the 'White Van' man; young men in Peugeots, and the 'Suited and Booted' in their lunch break. Now I'm not saying these people don't have children of whatever age, but at that moment that I wanted to park in one, with one or both of MY children on board, they don't have any children with them! I just wanted to yell at them. Most of the time – I don't yell.

I did drop the window down once and stopped behind one of the said culprits and said 'excuse me: I need to use that space! I have two little ones in here!'

I was either going to get ignored or receive a barrage of abuse and to be honest, I didn't think about it before I yelled out of the window. Instead, he just shrugged, smirked and walked into the store.

NOT FUNNY!!! I was seething...

Let's stop thinking about yelling and move on to the milestones a child reaches. These are BIG things at the time. To others, they don't mean a lot. To us – they are HUGE achievements.

'Look, he's sitting up on his own!'

'She's on the move' (bottom shuffling rather than crawling, but just as effective).

'Did you see that? He just used a spoon *on his own* and nothing went on me or the floor!'

'Did she just say something? I'm sure that was 'Daddy''.

'Oh my God, he's just done a wee on the potty – woohoo!!'

A major milestone is that of potty training. I won't go back to talking about poo again, but it gives me great pleasure in telling my experience of this here, as one person, who didn't have children at the time, once asked me not to post all over Facebook when mine was being potty trained. Apparently, 'no one wants to read about that sort of thing on there.'

Oh, but it's ok to bore everyone to death about how you went to the supermarket and overfilled your trolley?? Or how idyllic your life is when in fact you're just exaggerating to impress??

Potty training was not the horrendous experience I'd led myself to believe it would be. It was one of those things that for some reason I was dreading. I'd heard all sorts of stories about it taking weeks, sometimes months; heard all about the accidents children have during the process.

The 'do you use Pull-Ups or go straight to pants' dilemma. I'd also heard it was best to plan it when you AND baby were ready; that you couldn't go out anywhere for days and when you *were* ready to venture out, make sure you have a potty in the car for any side of the road stops. And if you knew when you got to your destination, e.g. The Shops, that you knew *exactly* where the toilets were.

The worries were endless. I had been scared into believing this was one of the worst things I would have to do!

So, I did what other neurotic mothers seemed to do and started reading. I read lots online (you'd think I'd learnt my lesson from my pregnancies, but no) and I also took some advice at the time, from Super Nanny, Jo Frost's book.

I did ask my Mum and also my Mother-in-law and they were quite helpful, although my Mother-In-Law then proceeded to ask me every weekend that we saw her when our son was about 18 months old if we'd sat him on the potty yet. Getting a little annoyed I ended up resorting in quoting the Health Visitor.

'He's not ready yet. He's not showing any signs of wanting to use the potty. And children aren't supposed to have their bladder or bowel control formed properly until they're over 2 years old, so anyone who tries it and *succeeds* before that age is very lucky and must have a genius child...'

Thankfully, I toned down the sarcasm in my voice as I said the last bit... She was just excited. She adored the children.

The months went by and when our eldest was 2 years and 9 months old, out of our group of five little treasures, he and one of the other boys were the last to be trained. Not that it was a competition, it never was with our 'gang' thankfully, but it was coming into the summer and I thought this was a better time to start trying. He could run around and not freeze his little bits off. I had to get MY arse in gear, get organised (there's that word again) and take the bull by the horns.

I had thought about whether to use the Pull-Ups trick or go straight to pants and opted for the easier option. Pull-Ups it was. Just in case there were accidents. We did all the things the books say to do – leave the potty in plain view; when at home - leave him with nothing on but a tee-shirt, and to keep asking him constantly if he needs a wee.

Thank God for laminate wood flooring that's all I can say! Although other than a couple of little puddles on the floor initially, he went and sat straight on the potty and did the business. In exactly a week, he'd got it! No horrible messes to clear up, we didn't have to inspect behind the dinning-room table or any corners in case he'd decided to do it there as some children can do. Apart from the first 2 days where I didn't go out at all, we did venture round to the Grandparents and it was fine! What on earth was I worried about??

Two pieces of advice I did take though: I went to a friend's house one evening during that week and a Nursery Nurse was there. Chatting to her, she suggested that I get him straight into pants and bypass the Pull-Ups. Boys tended to be lazy apparently - not all of them, but some. They needed their safety net pulled away. So, I took her advice. A brilliant piece of advice as it turns out.

I did take a little tip-off of another friend who told me to reduce his intake of liquid slightly. Don't worry, not enough to dehydrate him – just enough for him not to guzzle a bottle of water before we got in the car to go anywhere. It just made life a bit easier in the early weeks.

We did still have the stops in lay-bys though from time to time, sat on a potty while streams of cars go past. Thank goodness children don't know what dignity is at 3 years old.

So, he was dry during the day after a week. It took a bit longer at night but not months on end of continuous bed-wetting. We again took the advice of a book and 'lifted' him before we went to bed and sat him on the potty that we left at the end of the bed. Bless him, he hardly woke up, but woke just enough to know what was going on and went to the toilet in his potty then straight back to sleep after.

Eventually, we sat him on the toilet, and then a few months later he'd get himself up in the night, go to the toilet and take himself back to bed.

There's a lot to be said for leaving potty training until they're ready and not starting them too soon, as we'd discovered.

I'd been told that girls are easier to potty train than Boys. But our Son had been so easy! I wondered if we'd be lucky enough to have it easy with our Daughter when it was her turn.

Nope.

She was 2 years and 8 months old when we started training her. Unfortunately, it was November by this time and a bit colder! She certainly wasn't ready in the summer months, but we thought we may be able to get her trained so that she'd be dry for over Christmas.

Well, it was day one of training her, and it was clear she still wasn't ready. She sat on the potty – no problem. The only thing was it was *every* 5 minutes. Literally. Every 5 minutes 'Mummy I need a wee'.

'Ok, there you go.' And we'd sit there. And sit. And nothing would happen. And she'd stand up with red lines on her little bum from sitting too long, pull up her pants and leggings, and THEN she'd have a wee.

By the end of the day, she was stressed, and I was running out of clean clothes for her. So, I decided that enough was enough, and we'd leave it a few more weeks then try again.

We got Christmas out of the way and towards the end of January when she was nearly 3 years old, we tried again. We'd been talking about it with her for a while and I was determined to stick with it. Knowing how stubborn she was (was?? Still is!), we knew we may have a battle, but we were armed!

People advised me not to compare her to our Son's potty training because all kids are different. But it's human nature and you just can't help it sometimes. I had to try and forget that he was trained really quickly and just 'got it'. She may not.

After four days, we'd had several accidents and not many successes. We decided to go straight to the pants option and give the Pull-Ups a miss. We had Minnie Mouse pants, Disney Princess pants, Peppa Pig pants and Hello Kitty pants – we knew what she liked and there was no way she wouldn't choose one of those to wear each day!

On day five she was off to Nanny's house for the day while I went to work. I will admit I gave a small sigh of relief that I was doing something other than talking about poo, wee or toilets that day.

Unfortunately, they didn't have a great deal of success either. They were also on edge a bit with it all as they were trying to sell their house, and I did wonder if she set foot in their lounge that day or whether she was confined to the kitchen like a puppy in training!

For the following two days she was going to Nursery. I had forewarned them that she was being potty trained, and they reassured me not to worry and they would do what they do with all children going through it and take them every half an hour to the toilet.

'Shall we make you a sticker chart?' one of the girls asked her enthusiastically. 'We can make it with Princesses on!' Idea sold. To our Daughter AND me.

Why didn't I think of that for home? It was so obvious! It didn't cross my mind, but then the 'obvious' never does at the time when you need it the most...

And yes – after two days she'd had no accidents at Nursery. By the weekend she had it sorted, and she continued at home completely fine.

And so, the light at the end of the tunnel was getting brighter.

My Son was always Daddy's boy. He wanted Daddy all the time, whenever he was poorly, tired, hungry, everything. To the point that sometimes I'd get really upset and wonder why my Son doesn't want me?

Funny how it was always 'Mummy' though that he wanted in the middle of the night... I swear at 18 months he knew, and he was playing with my mind!

If I was worried about that, I needn't have been. As he got older, he became more loving towards me and I noticed this especially once he'd started school. What I should have done was made the most of him going to Daddy all the time, because when the little lady came along, boy did I know about having a clingy child!

For two and a half years, I had to prize her off me if I ever had to leave her anywhere. It got very wearing, especially as she'd also wake two to three times a night until that age, for no particular reason, and it was always me she wanted and me that could settle her. I was exhausted. It would always happen the night before I was due to go to work the next day! I needed buckets of coffee at work to keep me going.

Then all of a sudden, she started to come out of her shell and be more independent.

She also became more bossy, stroppy, aggravating to her brother, stubborn, funny (such a mimic), outgoing, and to my delight, more 'girlie'. Interesting times lay ahead.

We knew our son was good at using his initiative at the age of 2½ years.

He was always tall for his age and when he was still in his cot-bed, he'd stand there and we'd think to ourselves 'Mmm, we're going to have to lower that bed before long or he'll be climbing out of it.'

One morning, when there was no sound coming from his room at the regimental 7 am time he'd normally seem to wake up, I poked my head quietly round the door expecting to see him still fast asleep. It was still quite dark but as I looked harder, I realised as my stomach turned over, that he wasn't in his bed.

'Hello Mummy!' he said triumphantly.

'Oh my God – how did you get up there?'

He had placed <u>all</u> of his cuddly toys (there were many) at the end of his bed, piled them up, then climbed up and over the end onto the wooden changing unit and was sat there cross-legged, looking at a book. I made my husband get up and come and look.

'You know you were going to lower his bed?' I said matter-of-factly, 'can you have another think and do it quickly?'

Our Son continued with his 'good use of initiative' when, also about 2 years old, he was helping me clear out his wardrobe. I seemed to have an endless supply of baby hangers and wanted to move them into the spare room. He thought it would be good to help Mummy.

Now carrying a load of hangers is a bit noisy and awkward. Not for a 2-year-old. After taking the hangers two at a time backwards and forwards, he stopped, looked at the pile, assessed the job in hand, then took one of the hangers with a trouser rail on it, and hung loads of them on that! Then casually carried them all through to the bedroom. My Boy is a Genius!

He must get that from me.

In fact, I take that back, that's the sort of annoying yet sensible idea his Dad would come up with. He is his Father's Son.

Very effective though...

My two were both scared of the strangest things when they were little. We had the usual being scared of

Dogs, Spiders – yep quite understandable, bees and wasps – quite scary for little ones.

Flies – well, I guess they just thought every fly was a bee or a wasp, so we just had to very calmly say 'they won't hurt you – what do we say?'

'Shoo fly! Shoo!!'

'Good!'

However, we also had her being scared of cats – kittens to be precise. And puppies.

Wouldn't go near them. This was due to another delightful child telling them that all they want to do is scratch them if they went near them.

Thanks for that then – very helpful.

On one occasion, my daughter was sat on an outside toilet (yes some old houses still have these – they did have an inside toilet and bathroom too though if you're wondering!) when all of a sudden she screamed out and starting crying. There were full floods of tears everywhere.

'What's the matter? What's wrong?'

She wasn't saying. We thought she'd hurt herself or seen something horrendous. In the end, we had to take hold of her firmly and say 'what is it? What's the matter?'

'ANT!!!!!' she yelled, pointing to one about 3 feet away.

To a 3-year-old, clearly, that was horrific...

Chapter 23 – So What Happens Now?

Now - they are older.

Now - I appreciate the advantages of mine NOT being under the age of 3 years. We shouldn't wish them to be older, we quite liked their cuteness, dressing them in lovely little outfits *we* liked or parading them about to lots of 'awws' and 'ahhs' walking down the street hand in hand with us.

BUT, with age, comes great responsibility!

No - wrong phrase.

BUT, with age, comes great advantages! Let me enlighten/remind you:

- No Changing Bag packed with as much as you could cram in – the 'in case of' items;
- No pushchair to carry around in the car, allowing space again for shopping;
- No carrying of a potty in a plastic bag;
- Not having to plan the shopping route to include umpteen numbers of shops *with* toilets;
- Being able to use an escalator instead of a lift again;
- Saying 'yes' to impromptu gatherings, without having to think of sleep or feeding times;
- They eat when they're *given* food, not when they *demand* it;
- Less stressful social events. The list is endless.

We were once all invited to a BBQ a friend was having for their daughter's 3rd birthday party. They had a bouncy castle and trampoline for the children with games and food. Plenty of food and drink for the grown-ups too. Our children went off into the garden and played.

Yes, we had a conversation with other adults without having to either sit on the floor while doing it, limping about with a little person attached to my leg, pulling you in another direction. And, more shockingly, we found we were talking... to each other! In the same room!!

The art of conversation during the day, with each other, was returning...

Hang on though... there is a flip side to this!

- ❖ No pushchair - you've got nothing to hang your shopping on now and you have to resort to [deep breath in] *carrying it* again while trying to hold onto two little hands.
- ❖ No pushchair either for when the 'my feet hurt! /I'm tired!' cries start, within 10 minutes of walking anywhere;
- ❖ They get bored <u>very</u> easily when out shopping;
- ❖ They have voices. And they *know* how to use them. All the time. When you just want some peace and quiet, they get 'verbal diarrhoea'.
- ❖ Speaking of poo (sorry), even though you ask them if they need the toilet just before going out, sending them off to try just in case, they always need to go when you've just left the house, or the furthest away from a toilet ever;

- They want to do *everything* themselves. When you're in a hurry to get somewhere, they want to put on the most complicated shoes which they still haven't mastered themselves yet, but decide they want to learn how to do it at *that* very moment;
- They realise they do have a mind of their own, and they are going to use it to play with *your* mind instead, and test your patience to the limit;
- They want to choose their clothes – at 3 years old? I don't THINK so. Then when you only have 10 minutes to go before you have to leave the house, you give in saying 'oh fine - if you want to wear the Cinderella dress then you can if you want to, but not at the same time as your brother's Fire Fighter cape - you may get a bit hot, so just choose one!'

    'I can't wear these socks, Mummy, they don't match my skirt!'
    'They're white, it doesn't matter.'
    'Oh. Ok.'
    'I like your handbag Mummy'.
    'Do you?'
    'Yes, you can't have enough handbags'.
    Not sure where she picked that up from...
- Being sneaky: I've caught our youngest giving her older brother a sneaky shove, or a whack, or throwing something of his across the room. Then categorically denying it. At 3 years old, you'd expect a bit of that. It's the usual behaviour between siblings. But *nothing* was going to make her tell the truth. Leading on to...

- Stubbornness: we tried everything to persuade her to speak the truth, but she was NOT budging!

    'Did you throw that?'

    'Was it you?'

    'Just tell the truth'

    'We're not going to tell you off, we just want to know what happened'

    'If you threw it, it doesn't matter, just need you to tell the truth'

    'Now you mustn't lie, must you? So, tell the truth please'.

    Every. Single. Time we were met with a very convincing shaking 'no' of her head. Her Brother on the other hand was by now sat with his head in hands 'it was her Daddy, honestly, I'm not lying – look my tongue's not purple!' Oh, that old chestnut! Yep...

- Little white lies. Ok, we MAY have told them a little white lie ourselves about tongues turning purple if you lie. And a few more…

    'Oh, you've got too big for that toy now, shall we give it other babies so that they can enjoy playing with them?' *Translated to 'going to sell it now on Gumtree'.*

    'Can I have a ride on the Noddy Car?' she asks, as we're stood outside the supermarket. 'Maybe on the way out if we've got time'.

    And on the way out 'Erm, it's not working at the moment'.

    'Oh.' She said flatly. 'It's never working is it Mummy?'

I didn't want them to grow up too quickly. I'd noticed that my Daughter didn't stay a baby for very long. She did everything much quicker than her brother did, mainly because she just wanted to do the same as him. All the time.

It was still lovely to see the excitement on their faces planning Father Christmas' visit.

'Mummy? Mummy! The reindeer didn't eat all the carrot!'

'Oh, didn't they? Did the entire chocolate muffin get eaten?'

'Yes'.

Surprise surprise.

'Oh look, Father Christmas has delivered the exact same number of presents to both of us – that's good isn't it?'

I could see my son assessing both piles. Oh, thank God I remembered to count them.

Father Christmas was also used in bribery of course, as I'm sure is the case in most houses. We told each of ours that we needed to give their 'dummies' to Father Christmas as he needed them to give to other babies.

Thankfully, this worked. And thankfully I remembered to remove it from their beds in the night; otherwise, I don't know *what* we would've said had it still been there in the morning.

We also invented the Birthday Bear, who had the same rules as Father Christmas – if they weren't good, the Birthday Bear wouldn't come. *Is that just a bit mean?*

The Tooth Fairy visited of course.

'Did you know the teeth the Tooth Fairy collects, goes towards building their houses?' my Son informed me one day.

Although one day he came home from school, hadn't even *lost* his first baby tooth, and said rather disgruntled 'Mummy, today, Charlie said that the Tooth Fairy was your Mum and Dad! But I told him *that's not right!!'*

'Good for you' I said – annoyed that someone was trying to spoil it and he was still only in the Reception year at school!

'And I told the teacher and she said he was wrong too'.

That particular child also told my Son he was getting a Nintendo DS this year from Father Christmas. I had to sit him down and say that he *wasn't* getting one this year because... well... Erm... we didn't tell him in time that you wanted one. Phew!

And of course, there are the usual other white lies, some of which I blame my parents for by the way:

'If you make that face, the wind will change, and you'll stay that way';

'If you eat your crusts your hair will curl';

'If you pick your nose, your head will cave in';

'What meat's this Mummy?' 'Erm, it's dark chicken...'

'If you don't stay strapped in your car seat, the Policeman will arrest you';

Once the children were 3 years old, they became aware of their individuality. Their personalities were coming out – thick and fast!

They were very similar but also very different in other ways.

My daughter started coming out with things I wondered how on earth she knew at only 3 – but then she has an older brother, she just liked to copy all the time and she DID. NOT. MISS. A. THING.

Sat at a road junction, behind a car, taking a while to pull out, all is quiet in the car, and then a little voice pipes up 'Oh come on love! COME ON!! We've been sat here for *ages*.' Yes yes I know, it could've been a lot worse.

They get very clever and take you by surprise with it. They seem to have an answer for everything.

'Can I have some toast Mummy?'

'No, you're going to bed in 5 minutes.'

'Oh, please Mummy, please can I have some toast?'

'No, the Toaster's not working.'

'Oh, don't worry Mummy, I show you how it works, I'm good at fixing toasters'.

They also become very honest. One afternoon we'd gone round to see the Grandparents and their Aunty was there and she'd just got up, having got in at 3 am. She was sat in the lounge, VERY hung-over, clutching a glass of Alka-Seltzer.

'What does Auntie look like?!' their Granddad exclaimed.

'A scarecrow' my daughter said, as quick as you like.

She WAS having a bad-hair day. We all laughed. She just sat there. Looking a bit pale.

When the children were younger, they didn't tell you how much you'd miss them when you're apart from them. I had the odd wobble in the morning if I've been away from them all night, whether it was for work or a weekend away. And when you're *not* with them and hear another child cry or call 'Mummy', I automatically turned around to see if it was mine.

As they got older, their personalities evolved and they both developed traits which followed either me or my husband. That's still really fascinating to me. My Son has inherited his father's humour (God help me!), his sporting likes and skills – a bit of an all-rounder, *likes Maths* (no, I don't get why either), and can build and construct the most amazing things out of Lego.

My Daughter is very different and takes after me. She loves reading, writing, dislikes Maths, loves her swimming, dancing (that bit I never did – my legs were never built for dancing…), is very artistic and creative, and is an outgoing chatterbox.

'Try and enjoy them as children' my friend kept telling me. According to her, they're nicer under the age of 13.

Chapter 24 – A Word in Closing

I've covered quite a lot in this book about my experiences of becoming a Mum, and the children in their early years. As they grew older, we had the whole Primary School playground Mums 'thing', the sports days, the 'friendship issues', the fussy food era, the end of year shows, the Middle School moves, and everything in between.

My Son is now 16. Thankfully so far, he hasn't turned into a horrible teen, but I'm not counting my chickens just yet.

My daughter is 12 going on 18, but she is lovely, still a Mummy's girl and we enjoy each other's company, especially going shopping. Reeeeeeeally hoping this doesn't change, or am I just being naïve??

Together, mind you, the two of them bicker, just like I did with my Sister. And sometimes my Son takes it just that *little bit too far* and forgets she's not a tall athletic rugby playing teen like he is!

They both keep us busy, with school events and after school clubs. Then there's Karate, Scouts, Rugby, Athletics, Dancing and Swimming, and of course we, like thousands of other parents around the country, have to fit it all in around holding down our jobs and keeping a home.

The children have become strong, independent individuals and amongst the fun of being young, they've also had their fair share of sadness.

From the loss of a Grandparent, the sudden loss of a beloved Auntie and Godmother, and pets that have gone too, to the ups and downs of family life. All before they were teenagers.

My daughter went through unexpected major Liver surgery at 9 years old.

Unfortunately, they've also had to watch me go through diagnosis, surgeries, and treatment for Breast Cancer.

One of the worst times of my life of being a Mum.

I never expected to have to sit my young children down and tell them news like that.

It's one of those things people say, isn't it – that children are resilient.

They were correct. My children were amazing.

They had brilliant support from family, friends, the schools, the extra-curricular clubs. All helping them to keep their routine as normal as possible.

They saw me at my worst - poorly, bloated, hairless, lying in bed in a lot of pain, and I know this was so frightening for them. Especially having to stay in the hospital for a week at one point. They were so worried.

But they also saw me on my better days - up and about, doing the school runs when I could, adorning my lovely bright scarves, trying to make things 'normal' for them.

And seeing me getting better and stronger.

I am a Breast Cancer Survivor. And I don't take that for granted.

We are lucky to have two children who have manners, that chat to people and are sociable. They're helpful (at times!), funny and well behaved (in general).

We've always been able to go out in public with them to restaurants, without them running wild in between courses, or having tantrums in supermarkets.

Painting them as absolute angels, aren't I??

Ha! Not when they're together 24 hours a day they're not!!

Time apart is needed between them - regularly!

My son is now either out at weekends with friends, having his bit of freedom, or he can be found on "that damn PlayStation again!!".

This is in between homework, and his love of Sport.

My daughter, not quite old enough to go everywhere on her own yet, is more interested in music, dancing and chatting with friends on her phone, and saving up her pocket money for the next trip to the shops.

'Please don't buy any clothes for me anymore Mummy unless I'm with you. I'd like to choose myself now because I have specific tastes'.

And that was at 9 years old.

The experiences I describe in this book are mine, and I'm sure many women have experienced the same – or worse - or better.

Some of my experiences were funny.

Some not so much!

Becoming a Mum and reminiscing about my experiences has shown me that getting pregnant, staying pregnant, delivering a human being, and dealing with how life changed, was in no way as straight forward as I was told it would be.

They missed A LOT OUT!!

But then if we all knew what was coming, there'd be no surprises and it would all be so boring, wouldn't it?

The End

About the Author

Claire D Evans was born in Ascot, Berkshire, England and moved to Poole, Dorset in her teens with her parents and sister. An avid reader of Patricia Cornwell's crime fiction and reading up about fascinating and gruesome real-life crimes, her aspirations of becoming a Forensic Pathologist came a bit too late, so decided to stick with her Office based jobs instead. Claire has always enjoyed writing, from the odd poem, a blog, or generally writing notes to help in her day job.

Claire describes herself as a normal working people person, a 40-something with a love for music. Any spare time away from family activities include researching her family history and volunteering for Dorset Family History Society. And she has realised how much she loves a long walk now, especially by the Coast.

For the past 12 years, Claire has been working as an IT Technician/Service Desk Analyst and is now crossing off the things she promised herself she would do following serious illness – including publishing her first Memoir, which has been a long time in the making.

Printed in Great Britain
by Amazon